THE PARENTS' GUIDE TO KIDS' SPORTS

THE PARENTS' GUIDE TO KIDS' SPORTS

LEE R. SCHREIBER

A *Sports Illustrated For Kids* Book

Copyright © 1990 by The Time Inc. Magazine Company

All rights reserved. No part of this book may be reproduced in any form or by any electronic or mechanical means, including information storage and retrieval systems, without permission in writing from the publisher, except by a reviewer who may quote brief passages in a review.

First Edition

Library of Congress Cataloging–in–Publication Data

Schreiber, Lee R.
    The parents' guide to kids' sports / by Lee R. Schreiber. — 1st ed.
      p. cm.
    "A Sports illustrated for kids book."
    ISBN 0-316-77471-5
    1. Sports for children.   I. Title.
GV709.2.S376   1990
796'.01922—dc20   89–48236
                                                         CIP

SPORTS ILLUSTRATED FOR KIDS is a trademark of
THE TIME INC. MAGAZINE COMPANY

Sports Illustrated For Kids Books is a joint imprint of Little, Brown and Company and Warner Juvenile Books. This title is published in arrangement with Cloverdale Press Inc.

10 9 8 7 6 5 4 3 2 1

BP

For further information regarding this title, write to Little, Brown and Company, 34 Beacon Street, Boston, MA 02108

Published simultaneously in Canada
by Little, Brown & Company (Canada) Limited

Printed in the United States of America

ACKNOWLEDGMENTS

Special thanks to Richard Amdur, Donna Bassin, Anne Capeci, Tom Brennan, Mary Carillo, Michael Fischler, Alan Madison, John Monteleone, Lisa Reap, Tom Reap, Drew Schwartz, Ernie Vandeweghe and particularly the good doctor, Andy Price — all of whose contributions greatly facilitated my work on this project.

Personally, I'm much obliged to Meryl and Dennis, Keith and Joanne, Uncle Stan and Aunt Dolly (and all my aunts, uncles and cousins), Beth Bernstein, Phyllis Director, Coach Jan, the Pan-Hudson Rotisserie Baseball League (past and present), the Bizarro Summer House (past), Steve Allen, John Capouya, Lynne Einleger, Beth Filler, Roxanne Fischler, Granger and the twins, Neal Hirschfeld, Jeff and Andy, Michele S. Kay, the Kleins, the Kulawitzes, the Lenoks, Joe Marchetti, Mon and Joan, Jack Newman, the Olsbergs, Ron and Joan, Shoshana, Bill Simmons, the Skolnicks, Stan and Irma, Steven A. Strauss, Mike Vessio, Andrea Ziegler and Harv Zimmel — many of whom are parents, all of whom are still kids.

Interior design by: M. E. Morganteen

"The Young Athlete's Bill of Rights," pages 6-7: Reprinted by permission of the National Association for Sport & Physical Education, An Association of the American Alliance for Health, Physical Education, Recreation and Dance, Reston, VA.

"Pre–Participation Consultation" question-and-answer, pages 27-28: Reprinted by permission from "Preparticipation Sports Examination of the Child and Adolescent Athlete: Changing Views of an Old Ritual" by Dr. Thomas W. Rowland, *Pediatrician* (13: 3-9 / 1986), published by S. Karger AG, P.O. Box CH-4009 Basel, Switzerland.

"Foot Stuff," pages 36-37: Reprinted by permission of The Putnam Publishing Group from *Sport Health: The Complete Book of Athletic Injuries* by William Southmayd and Marshall Hoffman, © 1981.

"The Do's and Don'ts of Coaching," pages 51-52: Reprinted by permission of the Women's Sports Foundation, New York, NY.

"Guidelines for the Picky Eater," pages 74-75, and "Daily Food Guide/ Checklist for School-Age Kids," page 76: Reprinted by permission of Health Media of America, San Diego, CA.

"Sample Menu for Game Day," pages 82-83: Reprinted by permission from *The Official Little League Fitness Guide* by Dr. Frank W. Jobe and Diane Moynes, available from Champion Press, 555 East Hardy Street, Inglewood, CA 90301.

DEDICATION

This one's for — who else? — Mom and Dad and their first grandchild, the Kid.

Contents

Introduction

Part 1 — Getting Started   1

    Physiological and Emotional Development
    Open Growth Plates
    Sports Builds Character
    Choosing the Right Sport
    Competition
    Organized Sports
    Values and Ethics
    Sportsmanship
    Pre-Participation Exam
    Emotional Considerations
    Gearing Up
    Gym Class
    Professional Sports Camps

Part 2 — Parental Involvement   43

    Getting Involved
    Becoming an "Official" Coach
    Participation Beats Winning
    Coping with a Coach
    The Single Parent
    Family Participation
    Parents Who Push Too Hard
    What Parents Can Do to Keep Kids
      from Dropping Out

Part 3 — Girls in Sports   63

    Special Benefits for Girls
    Physiological Factors
    Equal Rights for Girls — It's the Law
    The Obstacles
    In It Together — Boys and Girls in Competition
    Girls' Injuries
    Girls and Contact Sports
    Giving Girls a Lift — Weight Training
    Nutrition for Girls

Part 4 — Shaping Up 73
Nutrition
Exercise

Part 5 — Injury Prevention and Treatment 95
A Glossary of Sports Injuries
Specific Youth Injuries
Contributing Factors
The Six *S* s of Injury Prevention
Visiting a Physician
Rehabilitation and Physical Therapy
Injuries in Contact Sports
Drug Treatment Shots
Burnout

Part 6 — A Sport-by-Sport Guide 109
Baseball
Basketball
Bicycling
Field Hockey
Football
Golf
Gymnastics
Ice Hockey
Martial Arts
Skiing
Soccer
Swimming
Tennis
Track and Field
Volleyball

Part 7 — Youth Sports Resources 129
Baseball and Softball
Coaching
Family Sports
Fitness
Football
Girls in Sports
Golf
Nutrition
Psychology
Soccer
Sports Medicine
Swimming
Tennis
Miscellaneous

Introduction

I grew up in the late 1950s and early '60s listening to stories of my father's athletic glory days in the rough-and-tumble schoolyards of Brooklyn, New York, during the '20s and '30s. I vowed then that when I grew up I wouldn't badger my poor kids with tales of my own sporting triumphs.

But I can't help it.

Like most people who reach a certain age, I often go back to those idealized, olden days of the past to review some treasured piece of my youth. Sports provide — for many men, and increasingly, for women — some of the most valued experiences of youth. And often the moment that moves us most is not necessarily the big catch that saved the game; it can just as easily be a little catch made while tossing a ball back and forth with Dad in the backyard.

A kid's first sports moment usually happens at home. A young girl wants to play catch or kick the can. A boy grabs a bat or a racket or even a parent's favorite hockey jersey out of the closet. Whenever, wherever and however it occurs, it is at that moment that the child enters — for better or for worse — the world of sports. It is a world filled with wonder and fear, loss and triumph. All young athletes need their parents' understanding, support and knowledge to ready them for the long distances ahead. And every parent needs guidance in this important aspect of childrearing.

The Parents' Guide to Kids' Sports is divided by design and concept into seven sections. The book is primarily written for parents of kids ages 8 – 13. The chronological differences are enumerated when appropriate, but most of the information and advice is universal — for boys and girls of any age.

The world of kids' sports has changed greatly over the years. There are fewer vacant lots and safe streets. There is more organization, more bureaucratization. There is probably much more parental involvement. Kids today are probably better equipped — not only with sneakers and balls and aluminum bats, but also with an increased awareness of the physiological and psychological benefits (and liabilities) of sports. They know the score.

Yet most kids still want what they have always wanted from sports: They want to have fun.

The Parents' Guide to Kids' Sports is not meant to replace coaches, physicians or therapists, or to tell parents how to raise their children. My function as author is simply to help parents ask the right questions: Is age eight too young to begin playing competitively? How much should winning be emphasized? When parents take on the job of Little League coach, how do they handle their own kids? Are girls' sports up to speed with boys' sports? What's the most effective meal before a game? When should it be eaten? How much should parents get involved in their kids' sporting life? In the end it's possible that more questions will be raised than answered.

So what is a parent to do in this complicated modern age? Well, of course the answers are complicated and simple. Some you can look up, and some are not found in any book.

Sports, as they say, is a lot like life: You listen, you learn. As a parent you push as gently as you can; you reinforce as positively as possible. And all the while you prepare your kids for the day when they will stand (or run or jog or jump) alone.

—L.R.S.

Part 1
Getting Started

"Being with friends, learning skills, experiencing the natural high of success, expressing individuality and learning to persist in tasks...The values learned through sports, especially hard work, hustle and determination, become an investment for the demands of life."
— *Chris Hopper,* **The Sports-Confident Child**

Any book on kids' sports has to start with the kids themselves. Who they are — physiologically, psychologically and socially — will indicate which sports might be best for them, when it would be best for them to become involved in those sports, and how intense their participation will be. Keep in mind that the interests of any given child can change as he enters the various stages of growth and development.

So before sending your sons and daughters off to Little League or tennis camp, it's important to know where they are in terms of their development, what their possibilities are for sports involvement, and what they will need to begin. It also pays to be aware of the many different bumps and curves on the road to healthy sports participation.

First and foremost, parents should remember this: Athletic skills can be taught to even the youngest children, but it's important not to push kids to go beyond their capabilities. Don't push. Don't rush. Don't worry. Each child develops and grows at his own pace.

PHYSIOLOGICAL AND EMOTIONAL DEVELOPMENT

Below is a list of the developmental stages — both physiological and emotional — that children typically pass through as they grow from birth to their teens. The list also includes the relevance of each stage as to sports participation. These are just general indicators. Each child is unique, and there's no one single age that serves as the precise starting time for particular activities.

Ages 0-6

During this period kids are mastering basic control over their bodies; developing coordination; and learning basic physical skills as they sit, stand, walk, etc. In these year "skill" is a very relative term. However, many of the movements a child learns naturally in his first years will develop into valuable assets in terms of athletics. For those parents who want to make the most of the child's natural development (and who, of course, will take care not to push their children beyond what they're capable of), here are a few "skills" that can be encouraged:

Slapping, Smacking and Pounding: As soon as a baby can begin to track objects with his or her eyes, a soft ball can be put into the crib to be slapped, smacked or pounded about.

Rolling: When the infant is capable of sitting up, he can roll a ball back and forth.

Kicking: At about one year, even before a child can walk, he can learn to kick. However most youngsters at this age need a helping hand or two to hold them up while they get their kicks. Since infants are still developing basic skills and coordination, be sure to use a brightly colored ball that is at least eight inches in diameter; this will make kicking easier for them. And the ball should be soft enough not to damage their tender feet.

Throwing: At two or three years, a child throws his first ball, doll, rattle — anything light enough to lift, but you will note a "flaw" in the motion. Most toddlers throw only with their arms and don't put any body motion behind it. Don't rush them to do more. It's too soon to teach curveballs or split-finger fastballs, although spit balls are allowed — in fact they're often hard to avoid! By $3^1/_2$, many children can throw with limited bodily rotation. By five or six, they start to step forward naturally and shift their weight with the throw.

Catching: Because it involves reflexes and reaction time, catching is more difficult than throwing for young children. In order for a five-year-old to handle a ball tossed at 15 feet-per-second (fairly softly) from 10 feet away, the child must begin a catching response virtually before the ball is released. Needless to say, most cannot. So instead of using a regular ball to teach your toddlers, play catch with them using a balloon. A balloon travels much more slowly, and a young child will have no difficulty getting under the balloon to catch it. At this age the important thing is not actually catching the balloon, but being in position to catch it. Studies have shown that kids must reach eight or nine before they are able to judge speed and the ultimate landing place of a ball. Proficiency will likely come by age eleven or twelve.

Hitting: As Baseball Hall-of-Famer Ted Williams likes to say, hitting requires more coordination and a faster reaction time than virtually any other athletic activity. As early as three or four, however, a child can begin taking batting practice — or to be more precise, swinging practice. Rather than have your splendid little splinter take a whack at a ball thrown freely in the air, tie a rubber ball or whiffle ball to the end of a rope that's suspended from a tree or overhang, and let your child swing away. As your child's skill level increases put the ball in motion before the swing. Later when proficiency builds even more, tie a knot in the middle of the rope; this will add a little "action" to the ball when you put it into motion, making it harder to hit. You can also try having your child hit a ball off a commercially available batting tee. This is easier than hitting a pitched ball.

Play Styles

Emotionally, kids can be fairly self-involved during these years. At around three or four, for instance, they are in the "parallel play" stage, in which only individual (as opposed to team or group) activities can be learned. During parallel play, one child will sit and play with his blocks while another child sits on the next stool playing with her blocks. They rarely help each other or interact. As they reach the upper end of the age range, however, at about five or six, these same kids will begin to interact. Instead of toiling in isolation, they will start to cooperate with each other.

While there are organized team sports for kids at the upper end of this age range (in some parts of the country, organized soccer and T-ball — using a batting tee — leagues begin at the age of five or six), the activities these kids tend to engage in often bear little resemblance to the sport as it's played by older children. Although there is a semblance of cooperative play, you will see most of these kids just running around haphazardly; children this age have little concept of organization and strategy. As a result, some leagues don't — and probably shouldn't — keep score.

When it comes to individual sports, kids' involvement can begin even earlier. In many Tiny Tots programs children as young as two participate in swimming and rudimentary gymnastics.

During these early years parents can be as creative as their imagination allows. In fact the wilder the activity, the more the child will enjoy it. Again rules are not the important thing for this age group; simply being active and learning basic athletic skills is perfect preparation for sports involvement later on.

Age 7

This year is a biggie, a real turning point in terms of both cognitive and psychological development. At about this time kids experience a growth spurt. The size of the brain increases to 90% of its total adult weight (compared to 25% at birth), and with this growth comes an increase in the part of the brain associated with muscle control. This results in the development of new physical abilities.

"In the preschool years, kids are clumsy. They throw a ball funny, they stagger a bit when they walk. But [then] they start to get graceful."
— *Dr. Sheldon White, professor of psychology, Harvard University*

Emotionally, age seven — the so-called "age of reason" — is a turning point. It is at about this time that children develop the understanding and desire to deal with the structure and framework of rules. They tend to cling to rules and organization.

Not surprisingly, team sports are perfect for these kids. While the age to begin sports participation is not etched in stone, it is around the seventh year that a child's interest in sports tends to become pronounced — when mental and physical capabilities begin to catch up with their level of enthusiasm and desire for athletic activity. Often there is a burgeoning preoccupation, even an obsession, with sports and physical games among kids; they seem to want to seek out every opportunity to test their newly-discovered skills.

Children at this age also begin to worry about success and failure, and sometimes their anxiety concerning performance may become self-critical. They are not always sensitive to this in other children, however; they often don't hesitate to ridicule each other, and can be downright cruel. Because of this, it is important to tailor team sports to take such things into account. Too much emphasis on competition and winning on the part of parents and coaches, for example, may have an unhealthy effect on kids. (For more discussion on this problem, turn to the subsection entitled "Competition," page 17.)

Ages 8-9

Kids in this age group are honing and building on the athletic skills made possible by the increased muscle control and coordination that occurs at around age seven. By this time kids are usually much better throwers and catchers, having developed greater proficiency in judging the speed and landing place of a ball.

The reasoning abilities of eight- and nine-year-olds are also sophisticated enough to enable them to concentrate more on rules and strategy,

> ## Kids In Sports
>
> In the United States, approximately 20 million children in the 8- to 16-year-old age group are involved in some form of organized sports activity. Of those, seven million children (representing half the boys and a quarter of the girls in that age range) are involved in some type of competitive, scholastic or organized sport during the school year.
>
> This is a time when many kids really come into their own. They truly understand the concepts of competition and strategy, and can play sports at a more sophisticated level. At this point it is more a child's personality than anything else that determines whether a team or individual sport would be preferable. (See also "Team vs. Individual Sports," page 15.) Some may have difficulty being one of many; others might feel awkward and self-conscious being put in the spotlight.

in addition to the athletic skills. They begin to empathize with each other, and tend to be nicer and more understanding. They are learning to compete without being nasty.

Ages 10-13

It is generally during this period that girls and boys undergo their adolescent growth spurt, as they reach puberty. During the growth spurt, while bodies are growing at an incredible rate, kids are often awkward physically; they don't quite know what to do with their gangly limbs. But as they grow more comfortable with their mature bodies, kids find they are capable of more strenuous and sustained athletic activity. Many kids who weren't particularly athletic before find that they have a new athletic grace and ability.

OPEN GROWTH PLATES

Growth plates — the soft cartilage located near the center of a child's bones — are responsible for the growth of the bones. The growth plates remain open until growth is complete and the bones have reached their full adult size. For most prepubescent kids — kids under or about 13 years old — the soft cartilage of the open growth plates can make bones prone to fracture, and the surrounding areas prone to other injuries. Thankfully, only about six to eight percent of kids participating in sports get fractures. (See also "Growth-plate Injuries," page 101.) Because the growth plates perform such a vital function, parents should be aware of the various stages of growth plate development and the potential impact of these injuries on sports participation.

Ages 6-7

At this age — presumably when sports participation is beginning for many children — the strength of a child's growth plates in relation to the accompanying ligaments and soft tissues is two-to-five times weaker than in adults. This makes these kids much more susceptible to injuries, particularly bone injuries. For a six- , seven- , or eight-year-old child, a growth-plate injury can increase the prospects of 1) serious leg-length discrepancy — an injury might cause a deficit of four or five inches in growth when the injury occurs at age 7, while at age 14 the same injury might only cause a quarter-inch differential; or 2) angular deformities in cases where there is partial arrest of growth on one side of the growth plate. Growth-plate injures can vary tremendously and therefore there is no one preventative measure parents and kids can take. General, overall safety precautions are the young athlete's best safeguard against growth-plate injury.

The Young Athlete's Bill of Rights

Noted sports psychologists Rainer Martens and Vern Seefeldt outline the following rights of every young person who participates in sports:

1. **The right to determine when to participate, in what sports, and to what degree of intensity and involvement.**

2. **The right to play in every game, regardless of degree of physical ability or the relative importance of the game in terms of league competition.**

3. **The right to be taught the fundamentals of the sport by a qualified teacher or coach, and to play on fields, courts and rinks that have been adjusted for children.**

4. The right to be coached by those who have been trained in, or who have been made aware of, the various stages of emotional and psychological development in children; to be treated on a level equivalent to emotional an physical maturity — not by standards of collegiate or professional sports.

5. The right to have a coach who places the child first, the team second, him- or herself third, and winning fourth; to feel free to laugh after a defeat, and to have fun participating even while playing on a losing team; to be able to use play as an opportunity to test life; not to be subjected to adult-imposed pressures to win.

6. The right to have a coach who is patient and supportive as opposed to one who believes in a harsh, negative, "professional" approach; to have a coach who takes time to work with each athlete, regardless of ability or potential, and who offers periodic evaluation of the child's physical and emotional growth as the season progresses.

7. The right to be treated as a member of a democracy rather than as a subject of a dictatorship; to voice opinions openly to the coach or parents without fear of negative repercussions.

8. The right to proper medical treatment; to play in a safe and supportive atmosphere.

9. The right to report to a coach or parent any physical pain or emotional concerns, such as fear or rejection, without fear of ridicule or loss of esteem.

10. The right to freedom from physical and emotional punishment by a parent or coach. Punishment leads to fear and inhibition. The purpose of sports should be to help a child grow, feel expansive and realize his or her potential.

Ages 9-11

This is a very key time of development, during which most children undergo their adolescent growth spurt. "As children grow, their muscles are basically being stretched by the bones growing," says Dr. Andrew Price, a pediatric orthopedic surgeon with New York University Hospital, in New York City. "When kids get to their adolescent growth spurt—around 10 to 12, depending on the child—the bones are growing, but the soft tissue such as muscles and ligaments are lagging behind. Because of that lag, there's decreased strength and flexibility—which can lead to a number of injuries, particularly around the knee."

At this stage, since the growth plates are nearer to closing, the bones themselves are not so vulnerable as they are in younger kids; it's the soft tissues that tend to be at risk.

Ages 12-13

The growth plates in 12- and 13-year-old kids are just about to close and are therefore much less vulnerable than they are in younger children. If a child does sustain a fracture through the growth plate, it's not as serious. Also since most kids at 12 have passed their adolescent growth spurt and are no longer growing at the incredible rate they were a few years earlier, the soft tissues are more stabilized and less prone to injury.

The Short Form — Adapting to Kid's Size

Most kids' sports are down-scaled versions of adult sports. But children are not just small adults. They're not nearly as fully formed — physically, mentally or emotionally. This means that for the most part they need and require rules and regulations designed specifically for them. Too often, rather than teach kids a more age-appropriate variation of a sport (T-ball is a notable exception), we try to teach them the adult game. Many sports can and should be tailored down to kids' size.

Children can often be resistant to this kind of tampering, however. No matter what their age, most kids want to be like the grownups. They see their favorite athletes on TV or at the ballpark, and they want to emulate them. Special care should be taken to show them that *their* version can be as meaningful and as much fun as the grownup game.

T-ball, as mentioned, is one example of tailoring a big-time sport into a modified, more appropriate game for preadolescents. Instead of swinging at a pitched ball, five- and six-year-old kids hit off of a tee, which can be adjusted to the height of the child. There are a few other adjustments — such as no bunting and no stealing — but kids do get a basic feel for the game of baseball.

Other games can also be easily modified to fit kids. For instance, Wilson Sporting Goods recently introduced "mr. pee wee tennis," a kit marketed for four- to eight-year-olds. The equipment included in the kit is designed to square off a regular-size tennis court into four small courts. Lew Brewer, a clinics administrator for the U.S. Tennis Association, says that Wilson's program is certainly a shot in the right direction. Smaller rackets, which are readily available for four- to eight-year-olds, are another great way to tailor the sport to younger players.

SPORTS BUILDS CHARACTER

The sports lexicon is rife with cliches, many of which are apt: "Sports is a microcosm ..." "Sports is a mirror ..." "Sports builds character ... "

Sports *does* build character. Perhaps even more important, sports *reveals* character — in kids and adults. Just watch a group of kids play basketball, and see if you can't immediately discern who looks to pass, who looks to shoot, who hollers at teammates when they make a mistake, who berates herself for the slightest error, who's the leader, who's eager to take the ball during crunch time, and so on.

In other words, by observing a child — or anyone else — compete in sports you will see

- How he copes with the pressure.

- How much of a team player he is, for example, whether he tends to grandstand, shy away from other players or work cooperatively with teammates.

- How he responds to failure or defeat — with tenacity, acceptance or rage, for example.

The list could go on and on.

Sports is an uncanny truth-detector. When there is pressure involved, as is usually the case, people tend to respond instinctively, and in doing so they reveal much about their personality.

Through a child's participation in sports, parents have a great opportunity both to understand their children better and to help guide their children's character growth in the most positive direction. A child's character is just beginning to form and develop. With proper guidance over time, the child who rants and raves on the field or court can learn to cope with stress and to develop a more even temper. And you can hope that that person will no longer be a crybaby on the basketball court at age 19.

Just because it has been said in every physical education class since creation doesn't make it less true: Sports participation is life preparation. It *does* help a child to overcome adversity, deal with pressure and act responsibly within a community. And often when the going gets tough, the tough *do* get going.

To most kids who become involved in sports certain universal benefits — physical, emotional and social — should accrue. In a nutshell, sports participation results in:

- Increased muscle strength and flexibility.

- A more lean body mass, and less fat.

- Improved cardiovascular efficiency.

- Improved body image, self-esteem, confidence.

- Increased ability to bond with other children.

- Improved sense of camaraderie and teamwork.

CHOOSING THE RIGHT SPORT

With so many different kinds of sports and so many different kinds of kids, choosing which sport to play might seem a gargantuan task. And in many ways it is. Basically this is a decision that will depend more on the child than anything else — on his personality and level of development.

"I feel very strongly that you let the child choose the sport."
— Dr. Andrew Price, pediatric orthopedic surgeon, New York University Hospital

Child psychologist Dr. Tom Reap believes that a parent must first see who the child is and evaluate everything that's going on in his life before determining how sports fit in. He says, "You can't take sports as a vacuum, dictating to your child 'This is good... or bad,' or 'This is what you should be doing.' It depends on the child."

Lisa Reap, Tom's wife and a psychologist with a private practice, says, "As a parent, the best thing you can do is expose your kid to a variety of activities. It's not up to the parent to determine what sport might be best for a kid. A parent should gently encourage the child to give sports a try. But the parent who says, 'I played football and now you have to play as well,' can do very major damage."

Parents should evaluate the child's strengths and abilities — both emotional and physical. They should consider the appropriateness of contact or collision sports. They should give some thought to the child's disposition and whether he is predisposed to a team or an individual sport. (All of these considerations are discussed in greater detail below.) Another factor to consider is whether the sport is something that the family can engage in. (See also "Family Participation," page 59.) Some kids want to do something that nobody in their family has any interest in, so they can go off and do it on their own — without interference. Other kids need the non-threatening support of the family in their sports life.

Occasionally a parent will have to disallow a child's choice of sports. Take the quintessential case of the scrawny, peach-fuzzed, 120-pound 12-year-old who wants to play tackle football. If the football program in his town is categorized by age and not weight, he might be competing against an almost-mustached, pumped-up 200-pound 12-year-old. Needless to say, this would not be a good idea.

In addition to thinking about which particular sport to participate in, some thought should go into the child's expectations of sports in general. What are his reasons to become involved? Is it to develop new talents? To make new friends? To become more independent? To be part of a team effort? To have fun? To become a superstar and earn a zillion dollars?

Any or all of the above are fine. The reasons will be different for each child. It's not a parent's job to be the constant voice of reason and reality. Encourage your kids; don't always censor their dreams. You might think you're protecting your children with platitudes of reasonableness and pragmatism. But after frequent nay-saying all the child hears is the nay. And what that child once thought was possible becomes an unrealistic expectation, a certain-to-fail, bound-to-be-disappointing pipe dream.

Choose-a-Sport Checklist

To help your child make the best decision, ask yourself the following questions about your child and where appropriate, ask the child directly:

- What are his particular interests?

- What are his particular talents?

- How independent is he?

- Does he like to socialize or does he prefer working and playing alone?

- Is he a risk-taker?

- Is he comfortable with contact and/or collision sports?

- Does he like a lot of freedom, or does he prefer some guidance?

- Does he prefer an individual or a team sport?

- How good an athlete is he?

- Are there any sports in particular that he likes to watch on TV or in person?

- Can he play this sport? (Sports should not exclude the handicapped; there are blind golfers, wheelchair-bound basketball players, deaf runners, and one-limbed skiers, to name just a few.)

- Is there a place nearby to play? If not, can facilities be reached by public transportation, or will someone have to drive him?

- Will he need lessons? If so, how readily available is instruction? How expensive?

In some cases the parent and child might need input from a teacher, a coach, a physician or a psychologist before making a choice. And then again, your child's choice is certainly not irrevocable; he can always try something else if the first choice doesn't work out.

Categories of Sports

Parents might find that breaking down sports into various categories is helpful in narrowing down their list of sports possibilities. Because different people make different distinctions, here are two methods of classification:

Dr. William B. Strong, a pediatric cardiologist at the Medical College of Georgia in Augusta, classifies sports in terms of their degree of physical involvement (although it should be noted that sports programs for younger kids — such as youth league hockey and football, for example — usually limit the amount of physical contact allowed):

Strenuous (contact): football, ice hockey, lacrosse (boys), rugby, wrestling, diving

Strenuous (limited contact): basketball, field hockey, lacrosse (girls), soccer, volleyball

Strenuous (noncontact): cross-country running, gymnastics, skiing, swimming, tennis, track and field

Moderately strenuous (noncontact): badminton, baseball (limited contact), golf, table tennis, horseback riding

Nonstrenuous (noncontact): archery, bowling, riflery

The classification system developed by sports psychologists Rainer Martens and Vern Seefeldt divides sports into three main categories, recommending an optimum age to begin participation in each:

Collision: football, ice hockey, lacrosse (boys), rugby — 10 years

Contact: basketball, soccer, baseball, wrestling — 8 years

Noncontact: swimming, tennis, track and field, badminton, golf, gymnastics, archery, bowling — 6 years

Hockey America has recently introduced nationwide rules prohibiting the use of body checking in hockey until the pee-wee level, which is for kids ages 12-13. However, there is still body contact when kids crash into each other by mistake.

There is virtually no physician or educator who recommends boxing as a sport of choice for any child!

Choosing a Lifetime Sport

It's hard enough for most kids to plan ahead 30 minutes, much less 30 years. But with a parent's gentle nudge some kids might want to give serious thought to choosing a sport they can play throughout their lives. Sports such as swimming, bicycling and running can be enjoyed by people of all ages. Many of the highly strenuous contact or collision sports, however, do not lend themselves to a lifetime of injury-free play. Chances are, even with advances in medical technology, today's kids will not be suiting up during their retirement years for a rugby or football team.

That's not to say that parents should dissuade their children from contact or collision sports. But children who are hell-bent on playing a contact or collision sport should probably be (again, gently) encouraged to have several more moderate backups.

Broadening Your Child's Horizons

Time and time again it's been stated that the choice of sport ultimately comes down to the child. But what about the parents who feel strongly that their son might benefit from an experience he resists?

Take the situation of an only child who feels uncomfortable in group situations. His parents might feel that he could benefit from a team sports experience, but he resists the idea.

"Listen to the child, but temper that with your own knowledge of him or her. Sometimes a parent can give the child several choices, knowing that any of them would be acceptable — physically or psychologically. In this way the child feels empowered and is encouraged to think independently, but you're still putting certain parameters around the choice."
— Dr. Tom Reap

If parents feel strongly that socialization and teamwork are important goals of sports participation, then it's perfectly okay to encourage their child to become involved in a group sport, even if he initially feels uncomfortable with the idea. Ask him to give it a try and if he still resists, respect his wishes. (See also "The Reluctant Athlete," page 32.)

Sports Single-mindedness

Some kids spend too much time involved in a particular sport, to the exclusion of other activities. A young girl who is determined to be a world-class gymnast and a boy who wants to be a pro football player might devote all of their time and energy to sports, forgetting that there's anything else in life.

The problem with this is that these kids often lag behind emotionally, socially and intellectually. Not only do they run the risk of burning out physically and emotionally, but lacking a well-rounded life experience, they often grow into emotionally immature adults. This is particularly true of individual sports, where there is no shared experience with other team members.

As child psychologist Lisa Reap has said, "I don't think being completely focused in any one area is ever good for a child. If you lose the ability to play that sport, you may think that you've lost everything. That's a lot of pressure to put on one particular area; the child's whole self-esteem is built around, say, gymnastics. But, in fact, their entire life is not gymnastics, even if they get up every morning at five. They go to school, they still interact with other kids. For some kids, this single-mindedness may become an escape, a way of retreating from the demands of the rest of the world, with this being the one area in which they have some control or mastery."

If a girl is set on becoming an Olympic athlete, it's important that she be exposed to other parts of life as well. That way, if she doesn't achieve her goal, she will know that there are other options in life, other areas where she can achieve competence.

According to Dr. Richard Lapchick, founder of the Center for the Study of Sports in Society at Northeastern University, the chances of a high school athlete in any sport making the professional sports ranks are 12,000 to 1. Parents should help kids recognize possible delusions, yet encourage children who have a chance to achieve their goals; help kids to think positively and follow their dreams, but also to prepare for unforeseen situations and possible failure. And even the word "failure" ought to be avoided. If the child has done his best, there should be a feeling of achievement, of experiencing something positive, and the satisfaction of having done something for the sheer love of it.

Team vs. Individual Sports

There is no firm answer to the question of whether team sports are better than individual sports or vice-versa. The considerations are different for each and every child. However parents should keep in mind certain developmental factors that might come into play, especially among younger kids.

For instance, as we have established earlier, a child of three in the parallel play stage, who is only capable of individual involvement, isn't going to be the best candidate for a team sport. But later on at around ages five to seven, when kids tend to want to be governed by structure and rules, team sports are ideal; they enable children to work cooperatively and have a common purpose without dealing with the "embarrassment" of being singled out. There's some comfort in being part of a group: The team loses or wins, not the individual child (although if a child drops the crucial fly ball in the bottom of the ninth, it can be plenty embarrassing).

Team sports help teach kids of any age valuable lessons. As players on a team kids learn that they are part of an entity greater than each child; each girl or boy has a responsibility to his or her teammates, both during practices and games and when scheduling — being part of a team means making sure one is available for practice when the rest of the team practices.

> *"If he asks me, I would prefer that my son play in a team sport, where he'd learn how to win and lose as part of a team, and enjoy the camaraderie of other kids....Tennis, in particular, is such a demanding and lonely game. There's no coaching during a match, no timeouts, no substitutions...it's all you out there."*
> — **Mary Carillo, sportscaster, former tennis champion**

As kids grow older, however, some may have difficulty being one of many. At that point individual sports may become more desirable. Performing individually, a child can be the star, with the focus entirely on him. Of course in individual sports kids must also learn to handle the responsibility of defeat; there is no one else to share it with (or blame it on). Individual sports are probably best for those kids who prefer to set their own pace and who have the self-discipline to practice by themselves.

Contact and Collision Sports

This is one of the more controversial aspects of kids' sports. When it comes to contact or collision sports, there is an entire body of professional opinion — much of which is conflicting:

"My personal opinion is that contact sports should be reserved for kids of about 12 or 13, around the onset of puberty, when the growth plates are closing. I have to temper that by saying: If my parents had said I couldn't play football when I was 10, I probably would've left home."
— **Dr. Andrew Price, pediatric orthopedic surgeon, New York University Hospital**

"I believe age 10 is the earliest most boys should begin playing tackle football."
— **Pat McInally, former National Football League punter, author of Moms & Dads, Kids & Sports**

Both men agree that there is a place for contact sports in childhood; only the parameters are in question.

Other experts, such as Mary E. Duquin, professor of sports psychology and sociology at the University of Pittsburgh, believe that there should be no contact sports at all — for anyone, at any age: "When you condone injury to another for the sake of a goal, you get into some moral issues. It's a great mentality for preparing people for war — but it is not the training for teaching empathy toward other people."

The fact is contact sports for children exist. It is up to parents and kids to review the evidence and decide for themselves at what age, if at all, it's O.K. to participate.

Naturally for kids of all ages it's important to ensure that contact and collision sports are made as safe as possible. This means using proper equipment (see also Part 6, "A Sport-By-Sport Guide," page 109), playing with a good knowledge of rules and with proper skills, and having adequate medical personnel on hand.

Age-based vs. Size-based Separation in Contact Sports

Chronological age, the usual method of classifying children, is not an appropriate criterion when it comes to sports, particularly contact and collision sports. If you take a group of children of the same age, some will simply be more advanced physiologically than others.

Because of this, most kids' football leagues are, or should be, categorized by weight and/or height. And even those yardsticks do not take into account the superior athlete's strength, agility, power and speed.

In addition to height and weight, it can also be helpful to make the distinction between prepubescent and pubescent children. In many sports, prepubescent children most likely will not be able to compete effectively against pubescent children.

COMPETITION

There are those who say that competition is unhealthy for children, that it hinders kids' ability to get along, increases their aggressiveness, places emphasis on winning rather than on a high quality of performance (thereby hindering learning), and creates a potentially harmful link between performance and self-worth. For these people the answer would be to completely eliminate competition from a child's world.

Most of us, however, must live in a world in which competition affects people at every level of society — and that includes society's youngest members. Whether competition in children's sports is good or bad, it exists. There are highly organized and competitive sports programs for kids as young as four, five and six years old. The object, I believe, should not be to eliminate competition, but to put it in perspective.

Instead of placing emphasis on competition and winning, kids should experience the competitive aspect of sports within a broader, more positive framework as they 1) learn to be an integral member of a team, 2) are encouraged to do their best and 3) learn to play as hard as they can, but always fairly. These experiences will give kids the capability of appreciating other aspects of team involvement, such as sharing, responsibility, persistence and coping with pressure.

That said, the question remains: At what age should free play — in which there is no competitive pressure to excel — end and more serious competition begin? The experts have differing opinions:

"For ages 3 to 10, the advantage of free play [versus organized sports] is that children play at their own level. It also permits the late bloomer, the more sensitive or clumsy child, to catch up."
—Dr. James Nicholas, sports medicine practitioner, director of the Nicholas Institute of Sports Medicine and Athletic Trauma at Lenox Hill Hospital in New York

"Children should have the widest possible experience of play — there are 'exercises' that even two-month-old infants can be given by their parents — but heavily organized competition with end-of-season championships should not be initiated before the age of 12, if then."
— *James A. Michener, in* **Sports in America**

"There is no one best age that can be recommended for all children to begin competing in sports. It depends on the individual and the sport. Children vary substantially in their rate of physical and psychologic maturation, some maturing earlier than others.... Parents and coaches must rely on their common sense to judge whether or not a particular child is ready to enter a competitive sport program. A useful indication for knowing if a child is ready to compete is the interest he or she expresses in participating, but this interest must not be the result of adult coercion."
— *Rainer Martens and Vern Seefeldt, sports psychologists, in* **Guidelines for Children's Sports** *(released in 1979 by the National Association for Sport & Physical Education)*

While there are no hard-and-fast rules concerning the issue of competition in children's sports, parents would do well to keep in mind the following:

Until about age eight, kids should be taught personal skill development, while at the same time be exposed to all the subsidiary benefits of sports — including the pleasures of playing and sharing a common experience with friends. Until they develop the capacity to empathize with each other, kids can be downright mean, and competition might only emphasize or increase any cruel behavior.

I have a friend who coaches his six-year-old son's soccer team in a league on Long Island, New York. These six-year-olds are just beginning to understand the concept of kicking the ball into the goal, and little else. But they love to run around. In this league the coaches basically put all the kids on the field at the same time, with virtually no concern about whether all 11 players are playing their proper positions. They throw out three balls, and the kids just run around and play, paying very little attention to strategy and positioning. They learn the rudiments — basically to run and kick (and occasionally head) the ball. But their primary goal is to have fun.

By eight or nine, kids no longer need to put down other kids to make themselves feel better. They're competing to make themselves feel better. And they start to think in terms of others — the team concept.

Between the ages of 8 and 10, children begin to develop a limited appreciation of another person's viewpoint, but it isn't until about 10–12 years old that kids truly empathize with others. Placing too much emphasis on competition without empathy may not be a great idea. However, starting at about age 8, the focus on individual skills can be augmented by some basic knowledge of rules as well as the concept of strategy.

After age 12 most children can reason at a basic level and are capable of truly empathizing with one another; they truly understand what competition means.

In many communities there are a variety of opportunities for children, each of which offers a different level of competition. For instance a school might offer intramural sports for those who wish to play primarily for enjoyment as well as interscholastic sports for those who want to compete on a more serious basis. Parents should encourage kids to seek out the alternative best suited to their needs and desires.

Cooperative Alternative Play

For those who would replace competitive sports with activities that foster peaceful interaction in society, are there any "team" options?

Absolutely. Dr. Terry Orlick, sports psychologist at the University of Ottawa in Canada and author of two books on non-competition *(The Cooperative Sports and Games Book* and *The Second Cooperative Sports and Games Book*) suggests that existing sports could be "cooperatively" altered as follows:

All-Touch Basketball: Each player on the court must touch the ball or receive a pass before anyone can take a shot. Once a shot is taken (or a basket is scored), the "all-touch" rule begins anew.

All-Position Football and All-Position Baseball: In both sports, a simple rotation system is used, with each player getting an equal opportunity to play every position; keeping score is optional.

Dr. Orlick also created special noncompetitive games that are not based on existing sports:

Lap, Sit, Step, Step, Step: A minimum of eight kids form a tight circle by standing shoulder to shoulder. They all turn to their right, grasp the waist of the person in front of them, and take one step to the center to tighten the circle. Each player then tries to sit on the knees (not thighs) of the person behind him — without falling over — thereby creating a sitting circle. The real fun begins when, while seated on one another's knees, the kids in the circle try to perform a variety of collective actions suggested by the participants: clapping hands, holding arms out to the side, touching the floor, and taking three steps forward, then three steps backward. Gravity generally wins out when the circle tries this last step.

(This game requires a high degree of physical coordination and is not recommended for children under eight years old.)

An important factor in all noncompetitive, or cooperative sports, Dr. Orlick asserts, is that all children should be "left in."

ORGANIZED SPORTS

"Kids today rarely pick up a ball and go to the park for a pickup game." "The sandlot games are all gone because all the vacant lots have been bulldozed for shopping malls." "There's no place for 'child's play' anymore." "Sports for kids has become too much like work."

Is this just a cranky lament, idealizing the glorious days and nights of their long-lost, perfect youth? Or in truth have organized sports for kids become over-organized programs — replete with regimentation and poor supervision — that are usually more of a chore than a pleasure?

The truth is, in my day there were more empty lots to play in. But they weren't entirely vacant; many were filled with broken bottles and construction debris. While there may have been more creative, untrammeled play years ago, the overabundance of choices resulting from greater organization of children's sports has created more opportunities for kids today.

For better or worse there has been a proliferation of organized sports in recent years — Little League baseball, soccer and pee wee hockey leagues, Tiny Tots swimming and gymnastics programs. Parents today seem to want to shield their kids from the hurts and the rejection they were subjected to during unsupervised sports play (although this is, of course, impossible). In some communities it's simply no longer safe to allow kids to run free, and thus organized sports become the only outlet. Or perhaps organized sports are a result of the increased number of single parents. Many parents work all day and don't have time to play with or even watch over their kids; rather than allow them to run off unsupervised, parents feel more comfortable having their kids participate in organized sports.

"The drawback [of all these leagues]," says Dr. Lawrence Elegant, chairman of the Sports Committee of the Illinois State Pediatric Society, "involves the question of whether the child is really enjoying it. Or is it a case of 'Here, make yourself busy for an hour and don't bother me'?"

The point of organized sports, as Dr. Elegant indicates, is not to have a glorified babysitting service. You can't just sign your kids up and leave them to the league's, or the coach's, devices. You can't always assume your youngsters are being given the proper tutelage and supervision.

What organized sports can do, on the other hand, is make participation more readily available for kids who don't excel, and who might otherwise not even play. According to child psychologist Dr. Tom Reap, "Kids who are never captains or chosen early in pickup games, or who may have always been picked last, might have been so traumatized by those neighborhood games that they eventually chose not to play. In a situation where a survival-of-the-fittest mentality reigns, there may have been a natural screening-out process for those kids who didn't want to face that humiliation. They may have just picked up one day and decided never to go back to the lot because they knew they wouldn't be picked."

Organized sports can be a great experience for kids. Parents who are interested in having their kids participate in a league sport probably won't have to look far to find out how, when and where to get involved. Take a look in the local paper or contact parents of other kids, the school gym teacher or someone involved in local government. Most likely the information will come to you from your child or other parents before you even go looking for it.

Overemphasis on Winning

Organized sports are fine, as long as they're not too organized. Playing well should be more important than whether the team wins or loses. The negative feeling that people have for organized sports usually arises from the overemphasis on winning. An obsession with winning at any cost (which usually trickles down to kids from a coach or a parent) is not the purpose of kids' sports. Most children would rather play on a losing team than sit on the bench of a winning one.

Jeffrey Vennell, director of sports and recreation at the University of Rochester, New York, observed the following scenario at a local kids' soccer game:

"This six-year-old stood almost alone on his half of the soccer field. The ball had been on the other half of the playing field for several minutes, defying the young children's often-futile attempts to kick it either into the goal or back to the other side. The boy, who knew that the rules prohibited him from crossing the midfield line to the area with all the action, got bored. A few moments later the coach, who was also the boy's father, looked in his son's direction and became angry.

"'What are you doing?' the coach yelled when he saw that the boy was upside down.

"'I'm doing a handstand, Dad,' the boy replied with a big grin. 'Pretty good, isn't it?'"

Vennell tells the story to make a point: "Most organized youth sport is overstructured and doesn't have enough play," he says. "Children need to learn how to play."

Different community programs have different perspectives on the importance of winning. Some don't keep track of statistics or league standings, while others go so far as to publish those things in the local newspaper. You have to do some research to find the program that most closely suits your child's needs.

Regardless of whether a particular parent or child will opt for a more or less competitive sport, parents should be sure their kids can put competition and winning in proper perspective. "It's important to talk to your child about the difference between being successful and winning," says Deborah I. Feltz, a sports psychologist at Michigan State University's Youth Sports Institute. "Children often have difficulty with that."

Make no mistake, winning is terrific. Few other activities showcase a kid's skills as openly as athletics, and few activities have such an immediate payoff. But competition also means learning how to lose; it's simply part of the game. By participating in sports — learning skills and the importance of playing well — boys and girls learn not to pin all their expectations and sense of success on winning; they learn to be less fearful of defeat, and to keep trying in spite of it. And it is hoped that they also learn another important lesson — how to be gracious in both defeat and victory.

Importance of a Coach

Virtually every adult who played a sport as a child can remember at least one coach from his or her youth:

"I was about seven or eight when I started Little League. Our coach was terrific: sensitive, warm, generous; he'd take us out for pizza after games. He made the game fun. Every Saturday practice was — literally — a picnic in the park. It was more than baseball; it was a social experience."
— Dr. Tom Reap

In his book, *The Hurried Child*, psychologist David Elkind says that school-age kids need someone who "senses their capabilities, gives them opportunities to work and reinforces their achievements." To the list of someones — which already includes teacher and parent — add the role of coach.

A coach can make or break a sport for a child. Even though a kid may be terrific at one sport, he may enjoy it less — or even stop playing altogether — if he has an insensitive coach. Coaches are important role models; they can have as much influence on kids as parents or teachers. The values taught by a coach are often the ones that the team — and each kid on the team — will reflect.

The subject of coaching receives far greater attention in Part 2, but a few things bear mentioning even at this early stage, when kids are just getting involved in organized athletics. The best coaches will sit the kids down before the season and tell them that the key is fun and participation, win or lose. They will play every child about equally in every game, and pat all children on the back, whether or not they excel. The best coaches foster the least threatening environment for kids so that each kid feels comfortable and rewarded, a valued part of the team. The best coaches are not stinting in their encouragement; they dispense positive reinforcement with every directive.

A coach, like a teacher or parent, must be aware of how each child responds in certain situations. Some kids feel more pain than others, some enjoy the pressure of a big moment, etc. The coach should try 1) not to be overcritical or judgmental; and 2) to teach empathy to the players so they won't berate an opponent or a teammate too unmercifully (the following week, it could be *their* turn to strike out with the bases loaded). All the kids soon realize that they will each have their turns: Sometimes they will be heroes, and sometimes they will be goats. A coach's job is to let the team know that either is O.K.

VALUES AND ETHICS

Most of us receive a basic foundation of values and ethics from our parents. Early in a child's development — as well as later, after most of the teachers and coaches have moved on — it is the parent who imbues the child with a set of values and ethics. Home is where the foundation lies.

I can't tell you how to bring up your kids. But I do want to relate this story about ethics in sports:

A few years ago I was watching a Georgetown-Syracuse basketball game with my brother, a Syracuse alumnus. I don't recall the exact situation, but I think Georgetown was down by two points with Syracuse inbounding the ball from underneath their basket. On the out-of-bounds play Georgetown center Patrick Ewing tried to draw an offensive foul. While holding onto the Syracuse player, Ewing fell backwards — with the other guy falling on top of him — presumably to get the "charging" call from the official. Ewing did not get the foul call, but for a split second it looked as if the official couldn't make up his mind who to call the foul on.

They kept showing the replay on TV, with the announcers saying, "What a heady play.... What a smart ballplayer...." My brother was furious. He — and virtually all Syracuse fans — thought it was a "dirty play."

The ethics of this case are more difficult to assess than the foul: Was it ethical of Ewing to draw the foul purposely? Some would say that college players are virtual pros, and they should be allowed to do almost anything, within the rules, to win. They maintain that this play is within the letter, if not quite the spirit, of the rules.

Even in kids' basketball games we have all seen it: One child is stuck out of bounds, trying to throw the ball into play with a kid from the opposing team in his face. Invariably a coach or a parent will yell, "Throw the ball at him!" In other words: If you can't do the right thing, do the only thing. Sure you might hurt the other child with this tactic, but hey, that's part of the game.

Or is it?

Is this what we want to teach our young children: that stretching the rules is O.K. if the end result is a victory? How important is winning, and how far should a player go in order to win? Should kids be taught this kind of thinking at age 8, 9 or 13? When, if ever, is it appropriate? Should the sport's rules simply be twisted to the team's benefit? Is the paramount desire to win — or to make sure each child has fun, participates and learns new skills? Is there an ethical code at work at all? If so, how far does it go?

There is no one set of answers, no single set of values. But these questions are certainly worth exploring and thinking about. And in doing so parents will probably be able to come up with a code that they and their children can live by.

Parents should keep in mind that the coach's view of fair play will factor heavily in their children's sports experience. Does the coach share your basic values (especially as concerns the questions above)?

It's important (especially with kids who are just starting out) for parents and coaches to talk about their respective value systems. If parents find that they are at odds with a coach, they should 1) consider placing their child on another team with a more compatible coach or 2) explain to their child how their values differ from the coach's, so that the child doesn't become too confused by any conflicting messages he might be picking up. (See also "Coping With A Coach," page 55.)

SPORTSMANSHIP

Sportsmanship is just another word for fair play and good manners, and at any and every age there are no winners without it. It's a concept that has nothing to do with ability or competitive spirit, but more with the way a player behaves. Does the third baseman argue over every ball and strike? Does the pitcher berate his fielders when they make an error? Do the first baseman and catcher joke easily with the opposing players or do they put on their grim, silent game face, refusing to make any contact whatsoever with the "enemy"?

In 1989 Tanner Munsey, a seven-year-old boy, received national coverage for the sportsmanship he exhibited during just two plays. While Tanner was playing first base in a T-ball game in Wellington, Florida, he fielded a ground ball and tried to tag the runner going from first to second base. The umpire, Laura Benson, called the runner out. Tanner went over to her and said, "Ma'am, I didn't tag the runner." Benson reversed her call, awarding the runner second base, and Tanner's coach awarded him the game ball for his honesty.

Two weeks later, with Benson again umpiring and Tanner now playing shortstop, a similar play occurred. Here's the account from *Sports Illustrated*:

"This time Benson thought Tanner had missed the tag on a runner going to third, and she called the runner safe. Tanner glanced at Benson and, without saying a word, flipped the ball to the catcher and returned to his position. Benson sensed something was wrong. 'Did you tag the runner?' she asked Tanner.

'Yes,' he replied.

"Benson then called the runner out. The opposing coaches protested until she explained what had happened two weeks earlier. Says Benson, 'If a kid is that honest, I have to give it to him. T-ball is supposed to be for the kids.'"

Sportsmanship Tips

Chris Hopper, author of *The Sports-Confident Child*, suggests the following guidelines for parents of young athletes:

- Encourage playing hard and fair but not deliberately breaking rules to gain an advantage.

- Discourage your child from making any negative comments to opponents before, during or after playing.

- Encourage your child to thank officials for their time and effort (especially when the officials are volunteers).

- Encourage your child to shake hands with opponents after the game and to thank them for competing.

PRE-PARTICIPATION EXAM

When I was growing up the pre-sports check-up was a simple routine: My pediatrician tapped my chest with a stethoscope and then smacked both knees with a little mallet. Unless he found a heart murmur or absolutely no reflexive response, the doctor signed my school health form, gave me a lollipop and sent me on my way. This ritual probably continued well into junior high school when I began playing interscholastic sports. Then the school doctor performed the same simple tests before signing the form.

Today, however, sports are more sophisticated than they used to be. Says Dr. Thomas Rowland of the Department of Pediatrics at Baystate Medical Center in Springfield, Massachusetts: "Newer issues such as injury prevention, body composition assessment and athlete education become important in not only assuring safe participation but also optimizing athletic performance."

Because of the increased sophistication, the scope of the pre-sports exam has enlarged. The newest trend is the multi-station exam, in which several doctors and/or physical therapists evaluate a number of physiological conditions, including:

Systemic hypertension: The normal rise of blood pressure is exaggerated in adolescents with systemic hypertension, and many sports pose a health risk to kids with this condition.

Structural cardiac disease: Kids with heart disease do not necessarily have to limit the amount or intensity of their sports participation, but a cardiologist should be consulted for any specific cautions or recommendations.

Irregular heart rate: Some, but not all, irregularities will put a child at risk during sports participation.

Dermatalogic disease: Skin infections can be easily spread in locker rooms; detecting and treating skin conditions is important, especially for contact sports.

Defective vision: Proper vision is essential for both safety and achieving optimum performance.

Neurologic disease: Depending on the disorder, a child may be steered away from a particular sport. A child who has had several concussions, for instance, should not play contact sports. Other conditions such as epilepsy, should not hinder sports participation, provided there is proper supervision and medical management.

Musculoskeletal anomalies: Musculoskeletal injuries are the most frequent complication of sports competition. Therefore it's vital to assess such things as body composition, level of physical maturity, flexibility and muscular strength.

Usually the pre-participation exam takes place at school (and is free of cost), with the child being ferried from one specialist to another. And if some condition or irregularity is discovered, the child is referred to the appropriate specialist for treatment.

Dr. Rowland maintains that multi-station examinations are "more expedient, sports-directed and inexpensive" than single-physician visits, and often more effective "in uncovering...musculoskeletal anomalies."

If it's financially feasible, a supplemental visit to the child's family doctor can also be beneficial. A private doctor who has known the child over a period of time will be more familiar with past medical history and will be in a better position to provide whatever long-term follow-up care is needed.

Pre-Participation Consultation

In his definitive study, "Changing Views of an Old Ritual," Dr. Thomas Rowland poses questions that parents and pediatricians often ask about physicals, and then he offers some answers:

Q: In this new era of sports medicine, are the goals of traditional evaluation still appropriate?

A: Some doctors consider the pre-participation exam an opportunity to provide full health screening, while others maintain that the purpose of the exam should be to identify new conditions that bear upon athletic participation.

Q: Are yearly health assessments of athletes necessary?

A: Most physicians agree that pre-sports exams are conducted too often. Annual evaluations to identify new conditions that would disqualify or modify athletic activity are highly unlikely to be productive. An initial physical exam when the athlete begins sports participation (usually junior high school) and another exam during high school is currently accepted as appropriate. Annual medical attention is still important, however, to review the medical history and assess rehabilitation of previous injuries.

Q: Who should be doing these examinations and in what setting?

A: Controversy surrounds the effectiveness of office-based versus multi-station evaluations. The private physician in the office setting has a better knowledge of the student's past medical history, may be aware of important psychosocial issues and can provide appropriate long-term, follow-up care. Multi-station examinations, on the other hand, possess the advantages of being more expedient, sports-directed and inexpensive.

In a comparative study of the two types of exams — single-physician visits vs. multiple (eight-station) examiners — greater frequencies of abnormalities were detected in the multi-station exam in the dental and musculoskeletal categories. The findings of abnormalities of spine, hips, thighs, knees and ankles were felt to be potentially important since those are the most common injuries that occur during athletic competition. Also, most of these abnormalities can be treated with physical therapy or other training measures.

Q: What are the true essentials of the evaluation?
A: Assessment of physical maturity, body composition, flexibility and muscular strength appear pertinent in both optimizing performance and injury prevention. Physically immature boys, for example, should be advised not to compete against their more physically-advanced peers.

EMOTIONAL CONSIDERATIONS

In addition to having your child undergo a comprehensive physical exam before beginning sports participation, it might also be a good idea to evaluate his psychological health.

Child psychologist Lisa Reap says, "We should take the time to listen to what children want, to who they are. Such an evaluation should determine: how kids handle stress and competition, how they perform under pressure, how they work with others versus working alone, their level of self-esteem.

"When kids have learning problems, you ... evaluate every aspect — cognitive, behavioral, physical — of their development so that you can pinpoint their strengths and weaknesses. It would be ideal if you could do the same thing in terms of sports.... There are such subtle things: How many times has the dyslexic child been shunted to the 'slow' class before the real problem was finally diagnosed?"

Below are a few emotional considerations which could factor into a child's sports participation. The list is not complete — no list could be — nor does it provide all the answers — again, that would be impossible — but it will give parents an idea of the types of issues that can come up. The key is to be aware, and to do everything possible to help avoid emotional pitfalls, and encourage positive, fulfilling participation.

Self-Esteem

According to most psychologists, the predominant emotional issue with kids is self-esteem. And so often, how kids feel about themselves comes from their parents. What kind of signals do the children receive? Are their parents positive — always encouraging the child with a smile? Or are they negative or withholding, demanding perfection and giving little or no encouragement?

It would be unfair to put the onus squarely on the parents, but the importance of being aware of how parental signals are interpreted and internalized by children cannot be overstated.

Kids with low self-esteem run the risk of pigeonholing all their energy, as in, "This is the only area that I'm good in, so this is all that I want to do" — or even, "I'm not good at anything." If children find an area of competence — in sports, music, whatever — it will probably go a long way toward enhancing their self-esteem.

For a child who's not doing very well in school or who feels unpopular, sports can become an arena in which to shine — and with so many different kinds of sports, just about every child should be able to find one he or she can enjoy and excel in. Through sports participation a child might experience a sense of mastery and confidence he feels he lacks in other areas. And this sense of accomplishment will probably help the child approach other tasks with greater confidence.

Developing Mastery and Confidence

We've all seen the shy little boy who suddenly "discovers" himself on the playing field and becomes a star. By mastering the skills of his sport, he develops confidence in himself. He comes to believe in himself, both on and off the field.

Sometimes this blossoming relates directly to physical development: The kid who is shorter than average all of a sudden has an incredible growth spurt that results in a greater proficiency in sports. Other times, proficiency comes as a result of hard work and persistence.

Success breeds success. Few of us are born with an innate, unshakable belief in our abilities. Most experts assert that this belief is developed over time. As soon as kids discover that they can conquer their anxiety and achieve a measure of success (however they define it — success is not necessarily linked to winning), they know it can be done again and again. Self-confidence is the by-product.

Coping with Rejection and Failure

Lisa Reap tells this story: "One of my clients, a 13-year-old boy, was the last one cut from his school tennis team. His mother said that when she picked him up afterwards, he had tears running down his face. In our session a week later he acted blase and said it didn't matter. His defenses had already started to build. And since it's still not macho or cool for boys to talk about these feelings of rejection, he was stuck with all these feelings.

"I had a hard time getting through to him until I said: 'Your mother told me that you looked in pain after you were cut.' Once he knew that I had this information, he was able to break down and say, 'Well, it would have been nice to make the team; but instead I've decided to join the Drama Club.' He withdrew entirely from competitive sports; that defeat really affected him.

"In this boy's case, his father was a tennis player. He had been teaching his son, and obviously had something invested in his offspring following in his footsteps. It was subtle, not that overt, but the boy was very clearly picking up that this was Dad's thing — and that not making the team was letting his father down. The therapist's job in this case is to let the father see how his response might affect the boy — and to encourage him to sit down and say to his son, 'Hey, no big deal... I still love you.' Fathers still have some difficulty getting in touch with their own feelings, much less their kids."

Why is it that some kids bounce back quickly from a failure, while others take it so much to heart? Again it's probably tied to self-esteem.

When children don't excel in sports or experience an "off" day on the field they can learn to take it in stride if they have a good sense of themselves, and if they know their parents are behind them no matter how well (or poorly) they perform. Knowing they've done the best they can, or that one bad day doesn't mean the end of the world, will mitigate the disappointment.

Stress and Pressure

Little League, for example, was a great experience for me. I still remember my heart beating faster when I went up to bat — especially in a big game. But playing in Little League taught me to deal with pressure, so managing stress became a positive experience. Even now, if I have to speak in front of a large crowd, my heart will beat faster; but I know that I'll get through it.

Competition can create anxiety and stress in some kids, particularly in those whose self-esteem is closely bound to winning and losing. Children involved in individual sports might feel that because they must perform without the support of a group their every mistake is magnified. Children involved in team sports, on the other hand, are subject to the criticism of the other kids on the team, the pressure of earning their approval. The sources of stress might vary, but it is invariably a very real part of children's sports.

Sometimes the kid who can't manage the stress withdraws. But what exactly is "managing stress"? More often than not, it has little to do with succeeding — getting the big hit or the key goal. Rather, it's a matter of putting one's feelings in perspective in order to be able to get through the situation, win or lose, without trauma. Parents should help their kid realize that every game is not a life-or-death situation, that win or lose, the child will still be important, wonderful, and special to Mom and Dad. (See also "Positive Reinforcement," page 44.)

> ### Stress Factors
>
> Here are a few things that can cause excessive stress in young athletes:
>
> - *A parent's or a coach's critical nature:* A child who receives a lot of criticism might very well start to "live down" to the negative comments (rather than live up to a more positive image).
>
> - *The limelight:* Many kids are uncomfortable with being singled out in any way — positively or negatively.
>
> - *Overemphasis on winning:* The player's sense of accomplishment and self-worth is tied to the results rather than the process.
>
> - *Unreasonable expectations:* Parents place excessive or unrealistic pressure on their kids to succeed — or in some cases merely to participate. Kids also do this to themselves.
>
> - *Inappropriate sport:* Some kids are better suited to individual sports rather than team sports or vice versa.

Burnout

This is a word — and a concept — that has only recently become part of the sports lexicon. And like much in the adult sports world, it is rapidly filtering down to kids. It is a psychological as well as a physiological problem.

As the title of this section indicates, we're only getting started. Therefore talk of burnout may be premature. But every parent should watch for signs of burnout — which include withdrawal, fatigue, boredom and overuse injuries and make sure that he doesn't push too hard or his child's sports career could be over before it even gets started. (See also "Burnout," page 107.) Too much competition at too young an age can result in too much stress, which in turn can lead to an early case of burnout.

Self-Talk

"You dope..." "You idiot..." "Why don't you open your eyes?"

With television using more sophisticated microphones to follow all the sports action, you can hear ill-tempered, rude tirades from athletes all the time. What parents and kids should realize is that when these athletes are not badgering officials with their litany of lousy language, chances are it's directed at themselves.

The tone and content of "self-talk" is usually self-critical, occasionally even self-loathing. Some athletes may use this kind of talk to psyche themselves up; but more often than not the athlete who yells at himself has already lost.

Negative thoughts elicit negative play; it's true in all sports. Young athletes should be encouraged to think of the last good shot or play, rather than the last bad one. And by thinking positively, kids have a better chance of duplicating the good plays. It's as simple as accentuating the positive: Don't demean or degrade yourself.

This is a message parents should convey to their kids while watching and helping them play, as well as by their own example. If your daughter sees you at the club tournament berating officials in your mixed-doubles tennis match, she may choose to emulate you. She may already have seen tennis player John McEnroe on television and have gotten the message that it's O.K. to scream at officials or even at yourself. Chances are she will behave this way and perhaps find herself losing continuously because of this behavior, until someone — either you, a coach or an opponent — sets her straight.

Help teach your children positive self-talk by always talking encouragingly to them: "O.K., you can do it." Or "Nice swing, honey." Also, remind your child to repeat the coach's instructions silently: "Head down, elbows up." "Keep your eye on the ball."

Teach your children well, and then try it yourself the next time you play a sport.

The Reluctant Athlete

Sports are incredibly diverse. There's probably a niche — and a sport — for every child. Initially, however, kids may shy away from participation, and in some cases, parents will have to get more directly involved in the decision-making process. As Emily Greenspan wrote in her book, *Little Winners:*

"Some parents won't nudge their children into sports at all for fear of being labeled pushy parents. But children often need a gentle shove: How many of us, adult or child, have loved anything we do from the start? Many champions who were lukewarm about their sports are now grateful that their parents made them get out and try. And many people whose parents steered them away from sports and competition are now resentful that they didn't have the opportunity to develop themselves athletically during childhood."

Usually a child's resistance has little to do with the sport itself; it tends to be an indication of problems the child is experiencing in other areas. These kids may be experiencing some peer problems; perhaps they fear participation because they don't want to deal with the issue of being liked or disliked, accepted or rejected. There may be any variety of circumstances at home and/or at school that are at the root of a child's reluctance.

Parents need to find out what is at the root of the problem and then think of how to improve the problem situation. Often sports involvement can help. A boy who worries about acceptance can be encouraged to play an individual sport such as tennis or golf. The satisfaction that can come from mastering the skills of the sport may help diminish his fears. The important thing is to be aware of what the real problem is, and to provide plenty of encouragement. (See also "Positive Reinforcement," on page 44.)

The Quitter

With a chronic quitter, for instance a boy who has difficulty finishing what he starts, it is often a good idea to make an agreement or contract with him before he starts participation. The child must agree to stick out the season, so that after two soccer practices, he can't just up and quit in frustration. As part of the contract, a parent might say, "After you finish this season, if you find that you still don't like it, then you don't have to play next year. But developing these skills takes time and patience, and you've got to give it a fair shot. I'm here to talk about it with you, even help you with your skills or if need be get someone else to help you practice."

Before devising a contract, however, parents should work with their child to try to find something the child has a chance at succeeding at. And again, providing emotional support and encouragement during the season is especially important for these youngsters.

The Unathletic Child

Not every kid is a natural athlete. But there's no reason for the unathletic child to miss out on the many benefits — and the good fun — to be had from sports.

> *"By the third grade, some kids are clearly ahead of others. They are more interested and successful. They play all the time, so they get better."*
> — **Rosemary Peterson, professor of child development, St. Mary's College, Moraga, California**

Kids who tend to lag behind in sports may decide it's just not worth it and give up. It's important to let a child know that he doesn't have to be a star to enjoy the experience. If children receive plenty of positive reinforcement and are not made to feel as though they are less valued or worthy than those who are more athletically adept, then the athletic experience will remain positive.

The Late Bloomer

Many kids who appear klutzy and unathletic in preadolescence may have a great deal of untapped potential. But by the time these youngsters come into their own, athletically speaking, they might already have been rechanneled in other directions by parents, coaches or other kids. At some point they became labeled or categorized as unathletic. And as anyone — child or adult — knows, it's tough to break that sort of label.

Kids who shun sports at 8, 10, or even 12 years of age may just be those whose skills have not yet developed or who have not been encouraged to play sports, and who may have lost interest. Maybe they are a little short on hormones or encouragement and need a little more time before shooting up in size — as well as in confidence and ability.

Don't be the one to tell a kid he can't play because he's not good enough, or that he will never become a pro so "Why bother?" I can tell you countless stories of 7-, 8-, and even 12- and 13-year-old kids who went out for team sports and who were ignored or cast aside by coaches because they hadn't matured yet. Just a few years later, when they hit their growth spurt, they were playing high school, college or even professional sports.

Perhaps the most famous example of a late bloomer is the extraordinary basketball player Michael Jordan of the Chicago Bulls. Jordan, who was originally cut from his junior varsity high school basketball team, went on to become one of the greatest basketball players of all time.

Dropping Out

There are some, albeit very few, children who may find that they just can't work through the stress and the pressure; no matter how hard they try, sports are not for them. They may have absolutely no interest in sports, and remain adamant about not wanting to be involved in sports.

As a parent you must listen to this child and abide by his desire, even if it doesn't coincide with what you want.

For these kids there are ways to be connected to sports without actually participating. A child who's not very good at baseball, for instance, might still enjoy the sport by watching the games on TV and collecting baseball cards. By becoming an expert, an authority who knows all the stats and the histories of the players, he can find his own place among other kids who like the sport, even if he doesn't play.

GEARING UP

This is an issue of great concern to parents, who naturally want to ensure that their kids are properly equipped. The importance of using the right gear cannot be overemphasized. It is vital both for preventing injuries and for encouraging a child's best, most fulfilling participation.

Most schools, and some organized sports programs, supply the necessary equipment for their young athletes. But undoubtedly there will be something the child needs that *isn't* supplied, and that Mom and Dad will have to go out and buy.

Before purchasing any sports equipment, be sure to ask your child's coach for recommendations. It's also advisable to consult your child's pediatrician. Otherwise there is no blanket rule as to what to buy or how much you should spend. But remember: The best equipment is not necessarily the most expensive. Unfortunately parents are often suckers for a quick pitch at the sporting goods store. "Don't you want the best for your child?" a salesperson might ask, holding up the most expensive sneaker in the store. Use common sense and a limit on spending.

There are of course certain items you won't want to scrimp on, especially protective gear for contact and collision sports, including helmets, padding, mouthpieces and protective goggles. Again, be sure to consult your child's coach before making a purchase.

The key word for all athletic equipment is fit. Parents often buy shoes or pants a size too big figuring that the kids will grow into them. This is a big mistake. Ill-fitting equipment can hinder a young athlete's optimum performance, and make him more prone to injuries.

In most sports (certainly those where contact is not an issue) perhaps the most important piece of equipment goes on the feet.

Footwear

I grew up believing that sneakers were the devil's footwear. My parents told me that sneakers lacked the support of shoes, that my feet would flatten if I wore them too much and that I'd develop "problems" when I got older.... Mom and Dad, I hate to contradict you in print. But you were wrong.

Sneakers are great, especially for kids. Just about all boys and girls like them, and they come in all different styles and colors. The best are light, flexible and sturdy. Certain sports call for specific kinds of sneakers or other footwear. Be sure to get what's recommended. Improper or inappropriate footwear — such as wearing metal cleats on pavement or hard-packed dirt; or using athletic shoes designed for natural grass on artificial turf; or playing tennis on hard courts with sneakers that were designed for Har-Tru, or clay, courts — can result in foot problems.

When choosing the "correct" shoe, ask coaches, shoe salespeople and physicians for tips. Again, make sure the shoe fits properly. The shoe should fit securely, but your child should be able to move his toes around freely. With shoes it's better to err on the side of bigger rather than smaller; an extra pair of socks can be worn to compensate for a minor disparity between foot and shoe, but the entire foot shouldn't be swimming around in open space. Most physicians and foot specialists recommend at least one extra pair of thick socks to protect the feet against blisters when the child is playing on a hardwood floor. Don't forget to bring an extra pair of socks to the shoe store.

Foot Stuff

Podiatrist Rob Roy McGregor enumerates eight key points for proper athletic-shoe fit (adapted from *Sport Health: The Complete Book of Athletic Injuries*, by Dr. William Southmayd and Marshall Hoffman):

1. *Heel height:* **Running with heels that are too low causes excessive pull on the calf muscles and Achilles tendon. This condition can be alleviated by raising the heel height with heel lifts or by buying new shoes with a higher heel.**
   (continued on next page)

2. *Heel cushions:* "Jogger's heel" is a bruise that can develop from a too-hard heel cushion. If the heel cushion is too soft, on the other hand, you can sink into your shoes, which could lessen the amount of rebound energy; this can often lead to fatigue.

3. *Heel stability:* The heel should be held in place by a "heel counter" at the back of the shoe to prevent excessive movement.

4. *Wedge support:* The rolling in or rolling out of the foot during running calls for support; the best support is achieved by adding a wedge from the heel to the ball area of the shoe.

5. *Floor-foot cushion:* The greatest amount of vertical force the foot must absorb is just behind the ball of the foot. To protect the foot, cushioning must be built into the shoe's sole. If you feel a "burning" in the ball of the foot, that usually means the sneaker is light on cushioning.

6. *Floor-foot flexibility:* A too-stiff sole, one that doesn't bend at the ball like the foot does, can cause excessive strain on the muscles in the foot and the leg, resulting in shinsplints, tendinitis or lower leg pain.

7. *Toe clearance:* There should be enough room to wiggle the toes easily. Otherwise feet could be more prone to irritations such as blisters, calluses, corns or "runner's toe" (a blood blister under the nail).

8. *Comfort:* Don't let a shoe salesman tell you, "The kid'll grow into them." If the shoes are not comfortable at the outset, don't buy them.

(More complete information on equipment is provided in Part 6, "A Sport-by-Sport Guide," page 109.)

GYM CLASS

Thirty years ago the militaristic, almost cartoonish, attitude of many gym teachers struck fear and loathing in even the most even-tempered girls and boys. If a child tried to skip P.E. (short for Physical Education) without a note from a doctor or a parent, the gym teacher probably would have told the offender to "drop and give me 20 [pushups]."

Thankfully today's increasingly enlightened and demilitarized gym teachers have made P.E. a less universally feared and loathed experience, even for the less adept athlete. The importance of good (and likable) gym classes to the well-being of kids has been recognized by health experts at the highest levels.

According to the President's Council on Physical Fitness and Sports gym class in the school has three main objectives:

1. To produce physically fit youth.
2. To educate young people concerning the essential nature of physical activity and its relationship to health, physical fitness and a more dynamic, productive life.
3. To give students the skills, knowledge and motivation to remain fit.

It is a sorry fact that for many schools it is now harder than ever to fulfill those objectives. Increasingly the bureaucrats have taken over schools' P.E. curriculums. In many cases reduced federal and state budgets have caused administrators to reduce physical education resources. Krys Spain, research and program development specialist for the President's Council, has said "When federal and state budgets are cut, the first thing that goes is gym class." This means fewer opportunities for kids to be physically active during the school day.

Physical Education Questionnaire

The President's Council on Physical Fitness and Sports asks parents and children to ask the following questions about the physical education provided by their school:

- Does your school provide at least one period per day of instruction in vigorous physical activity?

- Does each P.E. period include running, calisthenics and agility drills?

- Does your school offer instruction in lifetime sports such as tennis, swimming, golf, skiing or jogging?

- Does the school give a screening test to identify students who are weak, inflexible, overweight or uncoordinated?

- Are there special physical educational programs for the handicapped or underdeveloped?

- Are all students tested in physical fitness at least twice a year?

If your child's school system is not living up to the guidelines noted above, it may take some effort to bring the program up to an acceptable level. Check to see if local or state school codes mandate any or all of these things. If not, try speaking to a few school officials (concerned teachers, P.E. instructors, principals, members of the Board of Education) to have the school's program improved. And if you don't have luck on your own, try banding together with other parents; in all probability there will be others who share your concern, and usually there's greater power in greater numbers.

If for all your efforts you discover that nothing can be done, or that the school is already doing all that the community and/or the town budget allows, it's up to you to pick up the slack.

Make certain that your child gets at least half an hour of vigorous activity before and after school each day. Most children get their recommended daily fitness requirement from their regular routine — from running, jumping, climbing. Still, if they're not, many physicians believe it's a good practice to start them young before exercise becomes necessary.

(See also Part 4, "Shaping Up," page 73, for more information on exercise programs for kids.)

Because local school districts often establish their own athletic programs, as well as allocate a portion of the overall budgets, there is considerable disparity in the quality level of P.E. instruction among different locales, both within a state and between states. Some kids enjoy first-rate instruction and facilities, while others, whose districts work within budgetary constraints, must make do with rundown gyms and imagination — or, sometimes, with no gym at all. (Only two states — Illinois and New Jersey — require daily gym classes. In New York, although the Department of Education requires P.E. classes for all students, it does not stipulate any specific objectives.)

Overall, the results of budget cutbacks have been disastrous. According to the President's Council on Physical Fitness and Sports only a third of all elementary school-age children participate in a daily program of physical education (consisting of at least one school period of vigorous physical activity). One federally funded study, which examined the fitness of more than 13,000 American children from grades 1 to 12, found that through the fourth grade, most children take only 3.1 hours of physical education a week.

PROFESSIONAL SPORTS CAMPS

These days there are sports camps in all parts of the country, for kids of all ages, in just about every sport you can think of. "What is the reason for the tremendous popularity of these camps?" parents might well ask. "Why should I send my child to one?"

Sports camps can benefit kids by:

- Augmenting their learning skills in a particular sport.

- Introducing them to a new sport.

- Exposing them to different coaching philosophies, playing techniques and fundamentals.

- Giving them a chance to meet star professionals.

- Allowing them an opportunity to meet other children.

- Letting them measure and test their own abilities against a higher level of competition.

Most camps are reputable, reasonably priced and competently run, but some are a waste of money at any price. The best way for parents and kids to evaluate a camp is to research prospective choices carefully:

- Speak to other kids who have attended the camp in recent years.

- Talk to the parents of those kids.

- Request all the literature from each camp in order to compare price, location and instructional staff.

- When possible, visit the camp before you sign up.

- Ask your child's coach or instructor for input.

- Find out the ratio of campers to staff.

Keep in mind that the quality of sports camps is often mistakenly measured by the level of fame enjoyed by the coaches and athletes who are participating. Often the lesser-known camp (with lesser-known coaches and athletes) costs less and provides equally competent instruction. There is some truth to the supposition that Number Two will try harder — in this case to give each child high-quality, personalized instruction.

Part 2
Parental Involvement

"Parents are the key to an athlete' s experience and physical and personal development on and off the field....Young athletes should be praised when they do well, encouraged when they err, and consoled when they make major blunders or lose tough contests."
— **Pat McInally, former NFL punter, author of Moms & Dads, Kids & Sports**

"My parents gave me the freedom to find out for myself how good I could be. They encouraged me in sports at a time when it was not fashionable [for a girl] to be an athlete. They gave me their time. And I tell parents today that their youngsters need their encouragement and affection and help. These are the most important things parents can give their children."
—*Donna deVarona, former Olympic swimmer*

A child's involvement in sports can be a rough-and-tumble learning ground for parents. Doing the right thing — finding the time to get involved (but not too involved), interpreting kids' wishes, showing support, sorting through your own feelings about sports — isn't always easy. But it can be a lot of fun and a great opportunity to be actively involved in your kids' lives while at the same time watching them come into their own as they gain independence and mastery in sports.

GETTING INVOLVED

It's important for parents to participate in their children's sporting life and attend sporting events. Usually the *type* of involvement parents have in their children's sports activities is more important that the *amount* of that involvement. But it is important to be involved. Get behind your kids; show them that you think it's great that they're not only participating but excelling — in the sense of doing their best. Stress the area in which they are experiencing some mastery, and often that mastery will spill over into other areas.

The child who really wants his parents to watch him perform in sports and who feels that they don't come to practices or games often enough probably feels that his parents are not there for him in other ways, too. It might not be true, but the important thing is that the child *feels* that it's true. Parents need to be aware of and respond to this sort of need, especially if their children are having trouble in other areas. Feeling parental support in one area — in this case sports — can be vital.

> *"Kids need a parent to be there periodically, to watch them, encourage them, so the kid feels like the parent is part of his life. It's important. If a kid's father never shows up, that can be very upsetting. All the other kids' parents are there, and why isn't his? He wants the parent to see his progress, to give approval, encouragement. A kid cannot have too much approval or encouragement."*
> *— Dr. Michael Fischler, child psychologist*

Parents should try to attend most of the games, or as many as they can — as long as the child is comfortable with their presence. If you can't make a game or two for whatever reason, and your daughter is obviously disappointed, talk to her about it beforehand. Explain why you will miss the game. Tell her you'll be there in spirit, that you will be thinking of her. And try to make the next game.

There are, of course, kids who get extremely nervous when Mom and Dad are around, or who feel embarrassed when parents cheer too loudly or make a fuss. Some kids love the attention, but others think of sports as their own private thing. Either way, parents need to respect their kids' wishes.

Positive Reinforcement

There's no reason to scrimp on compliments with kids, and sports allow a very specific opportunity in which to give compliments. In the course of a game or practice there are dozens of opportunities to accentuate the positive, stressing a child's talents — even if his ability seems minimal. Find something good to say about the way your daughter hustles, or the fact that your son is so enthusiastic. Each time a child performs even the smallest task or function, it's an opportunity for an encouraging word or two: "Nice catch." "Way to go." Even when the child strikes out: "Good swing."

Eric Margenau, executive director of the Center for Sports Psychology in New York City, calls it the "apple-of-my-eye" dynamic, in which the parent gives unqualified acceptance and approval to the child. "There are many ego-building factors in childhood," says Margenau, "but the most crucial single one is that the child have the experience of knowing he or she is the greatest, the most important thing in a parent's life. If I could teach one thing to parents, it would be to communicate this message."

When it comes to providing encouragement and becoming involved, many issues can come into play that can be of particular relevance to parents of children who are involved in sports.

Letting Go

Perhaps the hardest thing for parents to do is to watch their children learn without helping, to let their kids make mistakes without interfering. But as former Olympic swimmer Donna deVarona says, "The most important way parents can help youngsters is to let them get to know themselves. And the only way they can do that is through life experiences. We live in a competitive society, and a lot of the values that help children grow as people can be found in sports. It is not the only place. Performance in any endeavor helps children grow. But sports does offer a great opportunity for growth and maturity."

Overinvolvement

Naturally parents want to give their kids support and encouragement, but there's a point at which parental involvement becomes intrusive.

If parents find that they are becoming too involved with their children's sporting life, it's very important for them to get to the root of their feelings and find out what it means for them. Is it important for their needs or for their children's? What is it that they're looking for in their children? Do they feel there was something they didn't get as a child, something that they're trying to make up for in their kids? Do they have fond memories of sports, memories that they now want their children to relive?

> *"Overinvolvement is ... far from beneficial to the child's character. What the parent intends as well-meaning protection, 'to save her from the hard knocks I had to endure,' may prevent the child from learning how to make decisions or handle problems competently—from growing up. It is not uncommon to witness some of the world's top athletes acting in juvenile, inappropriate ways. That's simply because they've never learned how to behave otherwise."*
> — *Linda Lewis Griffith, psychotherapist, specialist in athletic psychology*

Psychologist Lisa Reap says, "As a therapist, I want the parents to look for the meaning, sort out all the disappointments, hurts and anger that they might have felt as children and help them to realize: Your kids are not you. They may be similar. But don't try to make them you. You can't try to overcompensate for your shortcomings or disappointments."

Even the most sensitive and well-meaning parent can fall into the trap of mixing up her own needs with the needs of her children. Learning to separate your own expectations from those of your child, and dealing with them on your own (rather than putting your kid through hell) can help take the inappropriate focus — and all of the unreasonable pressures that can go with it — off the child. This separation should allow you to more readily view the sporting world from your kid's perspective and to determine what your son or daughter, not you, is getting out of sports. Consequently you will be more able to relax with your children and provide more genuine, no-strings-attached encouragement.

In *The Achieving Society*, David McClelland observed parents observing their children. McClelland gave children a number of tasks to be performed in front of their parents. Some parents, he noted, were tense and demanding, interfering immediately and trying to control their children by imposing their own egos; other parents were relaxed and supportive, encouraging and joking with their kids. Needless to say, the children of the latter group performed appreciably better.

In another study Robert Sears and his colleagues at Stanford University found that children of relaxed, supportive parents are usually "more honest, self-confident and mature" than offspring of the more demanding, withholding parents.

The benefits of avoiding overinvolvement are clear. What is less obvious is how parents can learn to sit back in the stands and enjoy watching their sons and daughters compete on the playing field or court *without* feeling compelled to run out and play the sport for their child.

Parents might have an easier time adopting a more relaxed, less intrusive approach to their children's sports if they keep in mind that the beauty of sports is that it fosters independence in kids. As kids master the skills of their sport and develop self-confidence, they begin thinking for themselves, learning how to cope with pressure. These are valuable assets in life (see also "Sports Builds Character," page 9), but children have to learn them on their own. Put simply, overinvolvement on the part of parents only hinders their children's ability to grow into mature, independent adults.

Perhaps a better word than involvement, and one that's certainly softer sounding than intervention, is guidance. Try not to command or demand. Guide your child. Kids shouldn't be constantly criticized or expected to perform under pressure at a level inappropriate to their age or development. Parents who sit in the stands and berate or criticize their own children, or other children, or coaches and umpires, set a terrible example. If on the other hand parents show the kids, the coaches and the umpires some respect, the kids will instinctively emulate their behavior.

Regardless of how good an example a parent sets, however, there will no doubt be some other mom or dad whose behavior is unnecessarily pushy or distracting. If you observe a particularly abusive or intrusive parent at the game, take your child aside and explain how Mr. Jones is having a bad day or just acting badly or whatever, and that his conduct is not appropriate.

Overprotectiveness

A natural desire is for parents to want to protect their kids from pain and rejection. Yet sports, like any other part of life, is often filled with both. There's no way that you can shield your child from the pain, rejection and disappointments in life, but you can help them learn to cope with these things in sports, and this can be an invaluable preparation for life.

When your daughter drops the ball in the bottom of the ninth, she is going to be devastated — particularly when her teammates don't try to make her feel better (and seven- and eight-year-old kids can be nasty). Parents might be tempted to respond to this situation by becoming over-involved — criticizing, pushing too hard, or yelling at other kids, coaches, etc. — as if somehow they could protect the child from having to go through these painful situations again.

This is impossible, of course. Parents can't (nor should they) watch over and protect their children 24 hours a day; they have to learn to let go. Parents would do better to provide encouragement and support, to help build their children's self-esteem so that they can make it through the painful moments with no lasting scars.

The "Unofficial Coach"

Some parents feel that attendance at their children's sporting events is enough. They leave the rest to the coaches, or to other parents who choose to become more involved. If they can, however, parents should try to reaffirm whatever instruction their kids are getting from coaches with some interaction of their own. Even for those parents who are not particularly athletic, there are ways of participating in their children's sports development. Just throwing and catching, for instance, will improve a child's skills — and will also help cement the parent-child relationship. Ask the coach what drills you can do with your kids to reinforce skills. It shouldn't take much time: Just 20 minutes in the backyard on a Sunday afternoon will suffice.

I remember that during football season my father and I would sit down in front of the TV every week and root for our favorite pro team, the New York Giants (as with most kids, Dad's favorite team became mine). At halftime we'd go out in the street and toss around the football. He'd crank it up, and I'd stretch out on the dead run to make some of the best catches of my life. Those fall afternoons with my father are among my most enduring and treasured childhood memories.

Parents might be surprised at the so-called "little things" that their kids never forget.

In addition to helping kids practice, or keeping up on the pros, some parents might even want to videotape drills, practices, or games, later replaying the tapes with their son or daughter. Kids will probably get a kick — along with some helpful pointers — from seeing themselves on video. But again it's important that parents do this for the child, rather than for themselves.

Some professional athletes still rely on their parents for advice. During the early years of his baseball career Mets' infielder Gregg Jefferies was said to rely more heavily on his father's hitting advice than on the advice of the team's hitting instructor. And Kent Hrbek of the Minnesota Twins credited a productive hitting spree to his mother, who noticed a mechanical glitch in his swing on TV and told him about it.

In addition to building physical skills, a parent can help the child emotionally — dealing with a difficult coach, coping with a tough loss, putting in perspective a particularly poorly played game. The inherent pressures of sports may crystalize or exacerbate any variety of problems. Parents should carefully monitor their kids for signs of stress or trouble brought on by sports participation. If the problems appear beyond the intuitive skills of a volunteer coach or a parent, a consultation with a child psychologist may be beneficial. (As already discussed in Part 1 under "Emotional Considerations," difficulties that arise during sports participation are often rooted in something other than the sport itself.)

BECOMING AN "OFFICIAL" COACH

This section applies primarily to league sports, in which younger kids — usually preadolescent — are involved.

Some parents may feel ill-equipped to handle a volunteer coaching job because of insufficient knowledge of sports in general or of a particular sport. In high school or college sports this might very well be true, but in most sports involving young children only a rudimentary knowledge is essential. Any parent can quickly pick up the fundamentals by reading books, viewing videotapes, talking to professional coaches (and/or other parents who coach), attending coaching workshops (youth baseball leagues throughout the United States sponsor clinics to teach volunteer coaches the rudiments of the game — hitting, pitching, fielding, overall strategy), or just watching athletic events on television. With most preadolescent kids, knowing how to deal with the kids themselves, rather than the Xs and Os of the sport, is crucial. Children will likely remember who you were and how you treated them long after they have forgotten the specific skills and drills that you taught them.

Parents shouldn't automatically assume that it's O.K. with their children that they coach them. Before making a commitment parents should discuss the idea with their children to determine the kids' receptiveness. Some kids might not want the added pressure or the attention that comes with being the coach's kid; perhaps they would rather be one of the group and blend in. No matter how even-handed the parent, certain kids may feel uncomfortable about having their mom or dad as their coach; for example, they might be less inclined to take risks when you're there to see them fail. Other kids will love the idea of having their parent as coach; it provides an opportunity to share something meaningful with their parents and to have them directly involved in their lives.

Sound out your child to see how she feels. And if your daughter decides she doesn't want you for a coach, respect that wish. If you still want to coach, you can volunteer in another league or for another sport in which your child isn't involved.

Tom Brennan, the father of two boys, has this to say about coaching Little League: "I got involved in coaching originally by accident. Like most parents I was being lazy and I didn't have the time or inclination to get that involved. But then the coach of my son's first team didn't show up for practice one day, and I happened to be there. As it turned out I really enjoyed working with the kids. At home afterwards I asked my son how he would feel if I coached his team. He liked the idea, so I just fell into it."

Some parents might decide to coach because they want in some way to be a child again, to re-experience the warm feelings they derived from sports when they were younger. That's fine, as long as these parents take special care not to force their own experiences and memories on their children.

Coaches are important role models for children, and they often wield a lot of influence over the young minds and bodies of the kids on their team. Therefore it's vital that parents examine their reasons for wanting to become a coach. They should try and recall their own experiences with a terrific and/or terrible coach when they were small and tremendously impressionable.

In addition, there are many questions that any prospective coach must ask herself:

- What is the optimum way to teach and encourage children — in terms of competition, sportsmanship, noninterference, and playing by the rules?

- How important is winning and losing?

- Should a coach treat kids who excel any differently than those who are simply enthusiastic?

- How can a coach engender enthusiasm in the unathletic as well as in the athletic child?

- How does a parent who's also a coach handle her own child in terms of the rest of the team?

- How much input should a coach accept from other parents who are not officially involved in the team?

There is no one correct answer to these questions. But considering these matters will help prospective coaches to pinpoint their expectations, evaluate their probable effectiveness as a coach and anticipate some of the issues that could arise during the playing season.

Taking the plunge and becoming a coach can be a very rewarding experience, but it also represents a serious commitment of time and energy, and it's not a decision to be made lightly.

Impartiality — Coaching Your Own Child

It's important for any parent who coaches to give some consideration to the question of how to treat her own child. Some parents tend to show favoritism when it comes to their kids. Others go too far in trying to show there's no favoritism, with the result that they they end up slighting their own kids. Or parents may put more pressure on their own kids — to be a role model, to perform above their capabilities, or to be better than the other kids on the team in order to set a good example.

Why? So the coach won't be embarrassed? Little League manager Tom Brennan tells this story:

"Whenever my son Doug would get up to bat, I'd be a nervous wreck. And so would he: I'd be standing next to him, yelling over to keep his eye on the ball, keep his elbow up, or whatever. And he'd be looking at me out of the corner of his eye — watching the opposing pitcher and me at the same time. *(continued on page 53)*

The Do's and Don'ts of Coaching

The Women's Sports Foundation, in its booklet, *Parent's Guide to Girls' Sports*, provides the following guidelines for coaches:

DO:

- Treat your kids the same as the other children on the team.

- Make it fun; the more kids enjoy sports, the more they'll want to play.

- Be patient; kids may initially be frightened or lack coordination, but with time and instruction they will learn.

- Make sure kids have the experience of performing the sport correctly; this develops pride as well as mastery.

- Use clear and comprehensive language that kids can understand (but don't talk down to them).

- Reduce the fear that kids may have by anticipating and lessening their anxiety; humor is always effective in accomplishing this, but sarcasm is not.

- Demonstrate and describe skills carefully so kids know what is being asked of them.

- Add skills in step-by-step increments so kids can see the correct execution.

- Remember that it's O.K. for kids to make mistakes; it means that they're trying.

- Allow kids to ask questions; this means they're thinking.

- Show respect for kids; treat them as though you are all learning together.

- Be positive and convince all players that they are making a contribution.

- Give each kid a sense of being special and important.

- Provide role models for your kids; expose them to other men and women in sports by attending school and college competitions, watching television programs, and reading sports and fitness magazines.

DON'T:

- Yell or scream at your kid or anyone else's.

- Condemn a kid for poor play or continue to bring up failures long after they have happened.

- Punish a kid for mistakes.... Punishment leads to withdrawal and (perhaps) to giving up.

- Point out kids' errors in front of others.

- Expect kids to learn things immediately.... With practice, they will improve.

- Expect kids to be pros.... Let them be kids — enjoying themselves and constantly improving.

- Expect kids to be immediately courageous.... It's natural to be frightened.

- Ridicule or make fun of a kid.... This only leads to further self-punishment.

- Compare kids to their siblings or to more talented kids on the team.

- Ignore your own child (in order to compensate for her being the coach's kid).... Each player on the team (including your daughter) wants to be important and special in your eyes.

- While in the presence of your child criticize or contradict your child's coach or referee.... This will cause confusion, poor performance, low morale and poor sportsmanship.

- Make sports all work and no fun.

"Finally my brother — who is also a coach — came up to me and said, 'When Doug gets up, why don't you walk out into leftfield. Get a drink of water. Anything. Just don't stand there and make you and your son crazy.' The irony of it was that I was a nervous kid when I played ball, and so I imagine my son to be equally nervous; I just want to make it easier for him — as most parents would. Anyway I took my brother's suggestion, and it's worked out fine."

It *is* possible to be fair to all children, without dispensing any special treatment. As difficult as it may be you must try and treat your own son or daughter like any other kid on the team. And if you find that it is impossible to do, you must quit the team (before your kid does).

Coping With Other Parents

Every league has its "problem parents" — mothers or fathers who yell a dozen different bits of advice out at the kid on the field: "Keep your head up!" "Watch the ball!" "Don't step in the bucket!" Faced with such comments, the child can all too easily become confused, between trying to remember what the coach said and now hearing all the new input from the stands. If she makes any contact at all with the ball, it should be considered a triumph.

If as coach you observe this scenario, take the parent aside for a private discussion: "Mrs. Voyce," you say, "great day for a game, huh? Listen, I don't know if you realize it or not, but I think you're making little Marion out there a tad jumpy. I don't know if you notice what I do when my kid gets up to bat. I walk away. Yeah, I know you just want to see her do well. But you're not doing either one of you any good. Believe me, I know. I'm a parent just like you. I get just as anxious and concerned when my kid comes up, but she has to do it on her own. It's tough, I know, but just back off a bit."

No Little League parent could reject such a compassionate pitch. If you point out that you're a parent, too, and that you're trying to do the right thing for *all* the kids — yours and theirs — most parents will understand.

Some problem parents won't be quieted that easily. These folks will badger, berate and bully coaches on strategy, on how much their kids should be playing — in essence, on how the team should be run.

Alan Madison, who coaches a middle school (fifth to eighth grade) basketball team in the New York City school system, says he has seen his share of bullying parents. "The key," he advises, "is to always keep your cool. I've had irate parents run up to me during a timeout or come and grab me at halftime. I usually stand there politely and listen. Or I tell them I will speak to them after the game. Then I try to explain why I'm doing what I'm doing. If they're still angry or have a problem, I tell them that if they're unhappy with my coaching, they can talk to the school principal. Most often, parents will listen to reason if I remain calm and consistent in my approach to both them and their kids."

If handled correctly, these "problem parents" can also be of assistance. Usually they are concerned and involved. The trick is to get them involved in a positive way — not only with their kid, but with the entire team. Ask if they want to help out in some way — even if it's just throwing the ball around at a Saturday afternoon practice. By making them feel that their input is valued, that they, too, can be part of the team, you allow most parents to relax. And you just might end up with a few extra helping hands when you need them.

PARTICIPATION BEATS WINNING

Most organized youth leagues begin each season with a parents' meeting — to discuss league rules, to establish the schedule and to see if any parents want to volunteer as coaches. Some league officials will broach the subject of winning and losing. They will say that the object of the game for each child is to participate, have fun and make new friends. Most will mean it. But regardless of the forcefulness of that message, there will always be some parents who are overly competitive (and who instill their competitiveness in their kids), and some coaches who place too great an emphasis on winning.

Little League coach Tom Brennan found that in the pee wee division — for six- and seven-year-olds — the feeling among participants and spectators was much different than that found in the higher leagues. "In pee wee baseball," he says, "everyone plays two innings, and after every groundball — whether it's caught or not — everybody cheers. The kids come up after the game and ask, 'Who won?' The emphasis is on learning skills, and the parents are much more relaxed about the competition."

In a perfect world that attitude would continue for four or five more years at least. Kids should be encouraged to play the game well — not merely to find ways to win. Take the "walk" in baseball, for example. At an early level, even with bases loaded, looking for a base-on ball is not going to help a child to learn hitting skills. We don't need 8- or 10-year-old tacticians. We need players, enthusiasts, kids who enjoy the game and who know how to hit and throw and catch; presumably they already know how to walk.

"I tell my players," says Brennan, "that I don't care if there are three balls, and you're the winning run. If you get a good pitch, swing. You're there to learn how to hit, to learn the game. And you're going to feel a lot better if you make contact." (At this level, there's a good chance that if a kid makes contact, he will get a hit.)

There are obviously a lot of coaches — even the good ones — who get caught up in having to win. In a close game their innate competitiveness just takes over (see also "Overemphasis On Winning," page 21). Tom Brennan tells of another game in which his team came from behind to score what would have been the winning run, until the other manager complained that the runner had missed third base. "Even if it were true," Brennan says, "it was too close to call. That's just not the spirit of the game. Our kids were devastated with this loss, after they had come from such a big deficit. I had to sit them down and give them a pep talk: 'Life isn't always fair. There's injustice in the world. The good don't always win....' All these platitudes. The parents wanted me to go to the commissioner of the league and protest, which I did. But the result stood, and the kids seemed to understand. Maybe the object lesson was ultimately more important to them than the game. But that stuff shouldn't happen in Little League."

Who's to say how much competition is too much? We have heard from some of the experts (see also "Competition," page 17). But this judgment really comes down to the parents and kids themselves, especially in league sports. How much competition does your child want? How much can she handle? If your child wants and is ready for a more competitive league or sport, you might want to try to find one. If on the other hand your child finds the overemphasis on winning too stressful, you should seek a less pressured situation.

COPING WITH A COACH

These days it's much harder than it used to be to get volunteer coaches. People are just too busy. So whenever someone is ready and willing to volunteer — even if that person is ill-equipped for the job — most organizations are not going to tell the person she can't coach. Many leagues have a review at the end of each season. But unless there's some egregious infraction committed by a coach — and usually insensitivity or over-competitiveness are not considered serious enough — she will be allowed to continue coaching.

It's up to the parents to evaluate volunteer coaches and decide whether or not they're right for their child, as well as for the job. Few parents would send their kids off, no questions asked, to spend several hours a week with a stranger. It's both advisable and appropriate to introduce yourself to your child's coach, and ask some questions:

- What do you want to accomplish this season?

- What do you expect from the team? From my child?

- What are your training rules?

- How important is winning?

- Do you emphasize winning over participation?

- Have you coached before? Where? When?

- How many of your kids from last season signed up to play this year?

Discuss these issues with the coach before the season begins so that there is a mutual understanding of everyone's expectations, and so there won't be any surprises. If you disagree with the coach's philosophy, you'll want to know about it up front, not after the fact.

Admittedly some of the more important questions can only be answered by observation, by attending practices and games to view the coach's methods first-hand. While watching, you might ask yourself these additional questions:

- How does the coach handle children?

- Is the coach positive or negative in approach?

- Does she seem to have a feel for kids?

- Does the coach give each child individual, personal attention?

- Are the coach's methods appropriate for this age level?

In addition, and most important, you should ask your child and some other team members about their feelings about the coach. Here are some typical questions:

- Do they like the coach? Do they fear the coach?

- Do they look forward to practice? Do they try to avoid practice?

- Do they talk about the coach a lot? If so, is it in a positive or negative way?

- Do they imitate the coach? If so, is it to show positive regard or negative regard?

If after all this you still have some concerns, you might want to speak directly to the coach — but only after your child okays it. Before approaching the coach you should examine your own feelings and motives in order to gain as objective an approach as possible. Talking to a third person, perhaps another parent, can help you accomplish this.

Approach the coach in a nonconfrontational manner. Find a private time and place in which to talk. Most coaches are parents, too. If you approach her in a polite, helpful way, speaking as one parent to another, the coach should be receptive to hearing constructive criticism and making the necessary changes.

If you and the coach still can't agree on a mutually beneficial solution to the problem, and if you feel that the coach's actions can be potentially harmful to your child, then seriously consider transferring your child to another team. Or if you decide to leave your child on the team, sit down with your son or daughter and explain those matters about which you and the coach have differing opinions. It's important to be very clear, so that the child doesn't get confused by any conflicting messages he or she receives from you and the coach.

THE SINGLE PARENT

This section is particularly, but not exclusively, geared to women — who might not have as much knowledge or interest in sports as their male counterparts.

Take the single mother. She works all day. She might not have time to watch over her kids when they're not in school. Rather than have them run about unattended, she probably would feel more secure knowing they are participating in sanctioned and supervised activities. If her children enjoy sports, league sports offer the ideal solution. For example, let's say this woman has two kids; one is playing baseball, the other, soccer. If and when she's around, she has to shuttle back and forth to practices and games. It's very difficult to be everything to both children: chauffeur, cheerleader and coach — not to mention breadwinner.

Even the busiest parents ought to be able to find some way of being involved in their kids' sports life. And once they do, there's every possibility that they will even enjoy it.

Single parents sometimes feel guilty that they're not around enough, but professionals claim that "enough" isn't necessarily "a lot." According to Dr. Tara Scanlan, professor of kinesiology at the University of California Los Angeles, "Single parents who feel very guilt-ridden because they can't attend all of their children's games may be perceived by those children as being very supportive and involved."

Again it's important for parents to separate their own feelings from their children's. If your kids feel you're doing just fine — and you should be able to tell — then lighten up on yourself. Likewise if they want increased involvement on your part, you should do your best to respond to that need, too.

Learning the Game — and the Lingo

Single parents may be at a disadvantage if they don't know very much about the sports their children are playing. The first step to sports literacy is learning the jargon and rules of the sport. This will enable previously uninitiated parents to enter their children's sports world more fully.

It's similar to any other new situation. You might feel that everyone but you is familiar with the routine, but don't be afraid to ask questions, however stupid they might seem; everyone was ignorant at some point. And try to put some spirit behind it. Everyone responds to an enthusiast.

Speak to everyone — neighbors, friends, the guy at the dry cleaners wearing a sports jersey — and pick their brains until there's nothing left to pick. Talk to other single parents whose children are involved in sports; treat the subject as a study group would, with each member focusing on a different aspect and then trading information. Watch plenty of sports on television, and write down any word or phrase you don't understand to look up later. (Admittedly some sportscasters are better than others in explaining the rudiments; unfortunately, most assume their audience already has a basic level of expertise.) Read pertinent books and sports magazines. If you have a VCR, you can buy or rent instructional videos (all kinds of videos are available in sports stores, video stores and libraries; just ask a salesperson for recommendations of tapes for the novice). And last but not least, speak to your child's coach. Most coaches are accustomed to dealing with single parents, and will probably be very patient and helpful.

It will be heavy going for a while; sports do have their share of esoteric rites and often arcane language. It may, for the uninitiated, seem like an alien world filled with gibberish and all sorts of mysterious locker room rituals. But once you understand the rudiments, the nuances will come.

A Woman in a Man's World

For those single mothers who haven't grown up with sports as an integral part of their life, there are some definite pluses. Women without a strong sports background are often much better "Little League parents" because they don't usually carry too much psychological baggage from their idealized days as youthful jocks. And while they may not understand all the subtleties of the game, this often makes them

The Time-Wise Parent

For any single or too-busy parent who works during the week and doesn't always have time to prepare the right snacks for her active children, Ann C. Grandjean, director of the International Center for Sports Nutrition in Omaha, Nebraska, has some advice. Ms. Grandjean says she spends several hours on the weekend at snack and meal preparation — in anticipation of a busy work week.

For snacks she refrigerates bags filled with fruits and vegetables, as well as cubed low-fat cheese. When fresh fruit is not available, canned fruit is almost as good. "Try to avoid heavy, sugar-based syrups," she says. When there is syrup, drain as much off as possible.

For meals, Grandjean says, "I put some low-fat cheese on English muffins and freeze them for a quick ready-to-heat pizza." Grandjean also recommends cooking a lean roast beef, turkey or chicken on the weekends, which can be eaten at various meals throughout the week. Other foods that lend themselves to being pre-cooked or prepared on the weekend include: rice, tomato sauce, lentils and other kinds of beans, chili, curry, macaroni and cheese, beef stew. "This way there is something always available during the week," she says.

---

less critical of their kids. They may root with unfettered enthusiasm on every play in which their kid is involved. And while there is a slight danger that an inopportune cheer will embarrass the child, unconditional applause can be a real plus, for the kid *and* for the team. (A short word of advice: As you become knowledgeable about sports, don't become more spare and specific with your cheering.)

FAMILY PARTICIPATION

Parents shouldn't automatically assume that their children's sports participation has to be separate from their own. They can, and should, consider the possibility of participating along with their youngsters. Sports can be a wonderful way for families to spend time together, skiing during weekends and vacations, taking the occasional afternoon bike ride together, or whatever. For example, John McEnroe, Sr., and John McEnroe, Jr., both learned to play tennis the same summer — when Junior was eight years old and Senior was ... well, a little older than that.

By actually engaging in the sport themselves, parents might give kids an added impetus to get involved. For children who need a gentle prod or push, family participation can be a particularly nonthreatening, noncompetitive way for them to become athletically active. (Other kids, as it has been noted elsewhere in this book, are determined to go off on their own and do their own thing; parents shouldn't force their children to participate if they are dead-set against it.)

However, parents who are planning sports activities for the family should keep in mind that the goal is as much to have fun as it is to maintain fitness and develop proficiency. Dr. Lawrence Elegant, chairman of the Sports Committee of the Illinois State Pediatric Society, says, "When you're doing fitness for kids, it has to be a fun situation rather than the old Army hup-hup-hup. There are a lot of things that can be fun. Swimming and bicycling are two primary ones, and they happen to be things amenable to whole-family participation."

Parents also need to make sure that whatever sport the family takes up is not too physically taxing on kids. Children under the age of 15 should not be encouraged to participate in overly strenuous activities such as marathon running just because their parents are involved.

PARENTS WHO PUSH TOO HARD

Eric Margenau, executive director of the Center for Sports Psychology in New York City, says, "I've never yet met a child under 12 who was seriously thinking about becoming a professional athlete — though some may give lip service to the idea. But I've met many parents who have that goal in mind for their child even before he has shown any interest in sports, let alone any particular talent."

All those kids who are up at 5 A.M. for practice every single day, 12 months a year (voluntarily or otherwise) are excellent candidates for burnout, psychologically and physically. At the appropriate time in kids' lives — certainly not before puberty — such a demanding training regimen may be acceptable. But not at 8 or 10 years old.

Again, parents need to keep a tight rein on their own expectations, and separate their own needs from those of their kids. Pushing too hard can only do children harm.

WHAT PARENTS CAN DO TO KEEP KIDS FROM DROPPING OUT

Often, the reasons kids give for dropping out of a sport have less to do with playing the game than with the way the sport is taught or coached, or with the type of encouragement kids receive. Sports psychologists who've studied the reasons that children drop out of sports have found that kids quit because of six kinds of problems:

1. *Not getting to play:* Studies show that 90% of kids would rather play on a losing team than sit on the bench of a winning team. This is not unique to youngsters. At any age if we are denied the right to participate in an activity, we turn our interests elsewhere. Some kids persist, however, waiting two or three years for the opportunity to play. And in many cases once their hormones catch up to their desires, these same kids become terrifically competitive and adept athletes.

2. *Negative reinforcement:* Initially, negative reinforcement and criticism may motivate athletes (or anyone, for that matter) to try harder. But over a period of time the constant barrage of criticism turns kids off.

3. *Mismatching:* Different maturation rates within the same age group can make chronological categorizing often unsafe and inequitable. Boys of the same age can differ by as much as five years in their anatomical or skeletal age. The kid on the short end of the maturation yardstick may just up and quit rather than face constant defeat by a more physically mature opponent.

4. *Psychological stress:* The joy kids have for sports can easily be dimmed when they feel overwhelming demands — either self-imposed or placed on kids by parents, coaches or peers. Kids often choose to quit rather than try and cope with the stress. In some cases it might not be such a bad idea to take a break from sports. In most cases, however, a sensitive adult — parent, coach, gym teacher — can help ease the child's stress.

5. *Failure:* "There is no single variable that produces more reliable effects in psychology than having individuals believe they failed," says sports psychologist Rainer Martens.

"Repeated failure generates anxiety, decreases motivation, results in performance decrements and destroys feelings of self-worth." This doesn't sound like much fun for anyone, much less for a kid who has not built up a reservoir of self-esteem from which to draw during tough times. Again it's up to the adults — folks who presumably have had years of experience and awareness in constructing their own storehouses of self-worth — to disabuse kids of this dangerous notion of failure.

6. *Overorganization:* Who can blame a kid for wanting to run or play freely, unencumbered by the rules and regimentation of organized sports? Fun is the most powerful incentive that draws kids to sports. Overorganization can take the fun out of sports. Understandably this can cause children to turn to other activities.

Most of these situations are preventable. Certainly there is plenty parents can do to keep their kids from falling prey to these situations. Be aware, watch for signs of discontent and do all you can to right those situations you feel are harmful to your child. Do all you can to make sports a positive experience.

Of course there are also children who do their best — and receive a lot of encouragement — and who simply do not enjoy sports. Once a youngster has given sports a fair chance, a parent should accept and respect her desire not to continue sports participation. Chances are, they will be much happier and more successful putting their energy into other pursuits.

Part 3

Girls In Sports

"Sports give you a genuine appreciation of your body. As an athlete, you are less likely to be pressured by the images of female appearance that our society provides via advertisements and the media, because your concern with health and strength overrides the latest beauty trend. Sports let you get to know your body and give you more confidence in it."
— *Linda Lewis Griffith, psychotherapist who specializes in athletic psychology*

"In the past, the main place where girls could be successful was school. By participating in sports, girls can get into a new environment.... It's a place where more girls can succeed."
— *Dr. Tara Scanlan, sports psychologist in the Department of Kinesiology at the University of California Los Angeles*

We have already established that children can gain considerably from their participation in sports, that athletic involvement generally results in increased muscle strength and flexibility; improved lean body mass (a higher ratio of muscle to fat); greater cardiovascular efficiency; enhanced body image, self-esteem and confidence; greater ability to overcome adversity and cope with pressure; bonding with other children and making new friends.

SPECIAL BENEFITS FOR GIRLS

It is indeed true that one of the singular benefits of sports to girls is that it gives them one more area in which to succeed (success being defined by competence and fulfillment, rather than by winning). Athletic involvement provides girls with an opportunity to break through traditional female myths linking accomplishment with looks and beauty; it frees them to prove themselves according to the same standards as boys.

In other words kids' sports involvement is great for general life preparedness. This is as true for girls as it is for boys. And yet historically the sports arena has been primarily the domain of boys.

Until recently many sports were not considered appropriate for girls. As the American Academy of Pediatrics describes so well in its 1975 report, girls were "deprived of their rightful share in physical recreation and sports by traditional concepts about a socially acceptable feminine image, misconceptions about the extent to which females may safely participate in strenuous activity, and, in fact, society's whole previous notion about woman's role and her basic needs and her physical capabilities."

But why?

PHYSIOLOGICAL FACTORS

Until puberty there is little difference in height and weight between boys and girls. From about age 8 to age 12 girls run a couple of years ahead of their male classmates in hormonal development, and therefore tend to be larger.

Motor skill tests have also shown that until about age 12, boys and girls are very similar in terms of various athletic abilities. Even when it comes to throwing a softball — the one activity in which boys have consistently outdistanced girls (girls' tosses top out at barely half the distance of throws of boys of the same age) — both physiological and psychological experts cite "insufficient practice and experience" as reasons for the girls' poor showing. Take away the factors of practice and experience, the study indicates, and throwing capacity is about equal between the sexes. A subsequent study found that there was no difference in distance between the sexes for throws made by the nondominant arm.

Dr. Jack H. Wilmore, Department of Education, University of Arizona, has said, "The female has the same potential for strength development as the male of comparable size."

Menstrual Irregularities

This is an area of concern for athletically active girls, and kids and their parents should be aware of the facts.

Studies suggest that female athletes competing in active sports such as gymnastics, long-distance running, figure skating, volleyball and racquet sports have an increased incidence of menstrual dysfunction. "The combination of low percent body fat, high energy output and stress" says Dr. S. Jean Emans, "has been associated with delayed menarche [the onset of menstruation] and menstrual irregularity in many sports. [However,] in most studies, swimmers have been an exception to the trend and have reported a menarche similar to the general population."

In a study conducted after the Montreal Olympics in 1976 it was found that the mean age for menarche was 13.1 for swimmers, 14.3 for runners, and 14.5 for gymnasts (compared to about 12.5 for "normal" girls).

This does not mean that athletic participation is unhealthy for girls, far from it. But parents of extremely active girls should consult a doctor or a sports expert to be sure they're aware of all the possible effects of sports participation.

EQUAL RIGHTS FOR GIRLS — IT'S THE LAW

The enactment by the U.S. Congress of the Title IX Educational Assistance Act of 1972 was an important first step in creating equality for girls in sports. Title IX, as this act is commonly known, called for equal athletic program support for both men and women in the nation's schools.

In 1975 the American Academy of Pediatrics responded to the changes effected by Title IX with the following basic guidelines for girls in sports:

- There's no reason before puberty to separate children by sex in sports, physical education and recreational activities.

- Girls can compete against boys in any sport if they are suitably matched for size, weight and degree of physical maturation and skill.

- Not only can girls achieve high levels of physical fitness through strenuous conditioning, in the process improving their agility, strength, endurance, appearance and sense of psychic well-being; it is also a fact that such activity has no unfavorable influence on menstruation, future pregnancy and childbirth.

- After reaching puberty girls should not participate against boys in heavy collision sports because of the serious risk of significant injury due to their lesser muscle mass per unit of body weight.

In the first four years following Title IX the number of high school girls' teams increased in number from 15,000 to 70,000. The dramatic growth continued during the 1980s, which saw a 700% increase in women's sports participation.

Increasing Numbers

In 1987 Wilson Sporting Goods Co. and the Women's Sports Foundation interviewed 1,004 parents and 513 girls (ages 7 to 18) in a nationwide survey of girls in sports. Here are some key findings:

- Ninety-seven percent of all parents believe that "sports and fitness activities provide important benefits to girls who participate."

- Eighty-nine percent of the girls surveyed plan to "make sports a part of their adult lives."

- Eighty-seven percent of today's moms and dads "generally accept the idea that sports are equally important for boys and girls... [with] little concern that sports may be 'unladylike.'"

- Eighty-two percent of the girls currently "participate in sports and fitness activities."

- Eighty-seven percent of 7- to 10-year-old girls are involved in sports (compared to 84% of 11- to 14-year-old girls, and 75% of 15- to 18-year-old girls).

- Seventy percent of the girls who participate in sports have parents who are involved in sports.

- Eighty-eight percent of the girls questioned said "other activities" distracted them from sports (39% cited "boys" in particular).

- Fifty-nine percent of the girls who drop out of sports cite the lack of time as one of the reasons for dropping out; 49% cite lack of skill; 30% say it's due to lack of opportunity.

THE OBSTACLES

Though Title IX made equal opportunity the letter of the law throughout the country, that spirit has not yet permeated all strata of American society. Former tennis champion Mary Carillo, who is now a television commentator, points out, "A lot of boys grow up wanting to be professional athletes. But I'm not convinced that little girls today can dream that dream. I mean, how can they? If there's a girl who's a good baseball player or soccer player, how far can she possibly go?

"The media have created a window for boys, and a ceiling for women. Girls watch professional sports on TV, and they only see women competing in a little tennis and some golf—that's it. There is no way that there will be leaps and bounds until women have the same exposure as men."

Girls are now competing successfully in national preadolescent soccer and T-ball (baseball modified for beginners) leagues, but that is a far cry from equality in all sports at all levels. It's still a sad fact of American life that there is not equal support for girls (and women) in sports. Factors such as coaching, facilities, training techniques and sports coverage in the media remain unequal between the sexes. In some places there are no girls' league sports at all, and women have had to form their own leagues in order to compete.

Little Ado

In 1989, Little League baseball celebrated its 50th anniversary. That same year another milestone received considerably less publicity: 15 years earlier—after a flurry of lawsuits, demonstrations and court orders—Little League Inc. dropped its hardball stance and agreed to let girls play in Little League sports.

By 1989 more than 200,000 girls were participating in Little League's softball program. It should be noted, however, that there was only about one girl per league in the 6 - to 12- year-old Little League baseball program.

The Stigma of Girls in Sports

The obstacles to equality have deep, tenacious roots in the traditional societal views of girls—even among women themselves. "When I first started running, I was so embarrassed [that] I walked when cars passed me. I'd pretend I was looking for flowers," says Joan Benoit, gold medalist in the 1984 Olympic marathon.

Today despite increased feminist awareness, girls are not given the same amount of personal latitude in their interests as boys. Psychologist Lisa Reap says, "The teasing usually begins at eight or nine with the beginning of some feminine identification and peer pressure. The girls who are very athletic, who dress in sneakers or aren't interested in the latest fashions, are ... very much ostracized and pegged as 'tomboys.' ... These 'jocky' girls are seen as wanting to be like the boys. Kids in general, much like adults, pigeonhole each other. They categorize you as the brain, the artist, the jock. And for a young, impressionable child, it's particularly hard to shake those categories.

"There's this antagonism: The boys have cooties, the girls have cooties....Few of their girlfriends are supportive, and their male opponents can be as cruel. Without strong support from the parents, young female athletes may withdraw from sports before they really give it their best effort."

And so girls who continue on in sports have the stigma of being associated with the cootie-ridden boys. Isn't that amazing? They have come up with a vaccine for polio and for the swine flu. And yet after all this time the scourge of cooties has yet to be eradicated from the list of childhood diseases.

There is still some negative connotation attached to "a very competitive female." Pejorative terminology is still tossed at the "pushy" or even "bitchy" girl who is merely exercising the same rough-and-tumble competitive instincts as the "assertive" or possibly "intense" boy. This double-talk bespeaks a still-present double standard.

The stigma of girls' participation in sports, and the resulting reduced involvement of women in sports (compared to men) creates another obstacle for young girls: the absence of a large number of successful role models for girls to look up to and imitate. Not surprisingly the negative effect of these perceptions can be very detrimental to girls' participation in sports. Bruce Watkins, a developmental psychologist and professor of sports management at the University of Michigan, found in a recent study of kids ages 8 – 17 that at around ages 11 through 13, when children start to make social comparisons, girls begin to drop out of sports. "Up through elementary school," Watkins says, "girls can be found participating in sports on an equal level with boys. [But] as boys mature physically and become stronger, girls see they do not have comparable strength or size, and they quit. Given more time to develop, they might improve their skills and be able to compete in the sport."

According to this same study, female athletes consistently rated themselves lower in ability than they should. This attitude was evident even in girls as early as the third grade, at an age when girls might be physically superior to boys. Watkins concluded that competitiveness seemed to develop earlier in boys than in girls, and is more obvious in boys. In addition he found that girls seemed reluctant to be in competition with boys.

What Can Parents Do?

Despite these gloomy statistics we all know that girls have every right to participate as fully as boys in sports and to develop their athletic abilities. The gratification and feelings of mastery that are the results of participation should allow girls to transcend any taunts they receive. But for the girls who don't have a clear sense of themselves and who are overly sensitive to criticism, the teasing can be very damaging. It can even make them drop out of sports entirely.

Because of the obstacles many girls face, it is doubly important that they receive proper encouragement from their parents, and plenty of it (see also "Positive Reinforcement," page 44). Make sure you give your daughters the same support as your sons when it comes to sports. Don't belittle their athletic efforts; let them know that you think their participation in any sport worthwhile and commendable.

IN IT TOGETHER — BOYS AND GIRLS IN COMPETITION

Before puberty there is no good physiological or psychological reason for boys and girls to be separated in physical education classes or in other sports participation. There's no reason at all for one gender's sports program to be any less strenuous than the other's.

Elementary school gym classes are commonly coed. At that age, however, kids mostly learn game-playing skills. When they branch off into more competitive athletics, in junior high and high school, gym classes — and teams — are usually comprised of a single gender. The argument for this separation is that on coed teams, even in noncontact sports, the boys will dominate. (In some cases rules of the game have even been diluted for the "weaker sex." National volleyball rules, for example, require boys to play with a higher net than girls.)

Many medical and physical education specialists are coming to believe that this emphasis on male-oriented sports should be softened. Not only does it exclude many students — less heavily built boys as well as girls — and glorify competition, but it also ignores the importance of instilling in all students good exercise habits.

There are some experts who assert that an extraordinarily developed, conditioned or adept female athlete can compete successfully with similarly conditioned boys of the same weight and height. According to Charles Corbin, professor of health and physical education at Arizona State University at Tempe, "If boys and girls are equally matched by age, ability, experience, height and weight, girls can play on boys' teams, and vice versa. It's more fun and [like] real life."

William Squires, professor of biology, health-fitness and nutrition at Texas Lutheran College-Seguin, holds a similar view. He maintains that in an enlightened society girls and boys could compete together: "You could have a coed basketball league and have the three best boys and three best girls on one team play another school's three best boys and girls."

In the real world this might not actually be the case — yet; but it is certainly something to work toward. And in the meantime there are sports — such as golf, tennis and running — that are easily played with boys and girls competing on the same team.

GIRLS' INJURIES

With girls now competing more in sports, against boys as well as among themselves, there has been increased interest and concern with the severity and frequency of injuries. Many people used to assume that having girls participate with boys would increase the likelihood of injuries. Thus far studies show this isn't true, that girls involved in the same sports as boys are not any more or less prone to injuries than boys.

That is not to say that girls don't need to do anything to protect themselves from injury; they do. Girls, like boys, should always wear the proper protective gear, make sure they are playing their sport properly, not overburden their bodies and check that there is adequate medical assistance available. (See also Part 5, "Injury Prevention and Treatment," page 95.) And naturally parents and kids should be aware of any injuries or conditions that are associated with a particular sport so that they can take any appropriate preventive measures. This will help ensure the most injury-free participation possible.

Girls in particular need to make sure they don't overburden their bodies. Since their bodies mature about a year or two before boys, they are often able to enter into serious competition at a younger age than boys. As a result many female Olympic or world-class athletes— particularly in sports such as gymnastics, swimming and tennis— may subject their bodies to tremendous stress at a young age. This can result in over-use injuries, such as spondylolysis or even burnout.

Therefore it's often a good idea to limit the range, length or repetition of particularly strenuous activities and/or motions; this will help to prevent overtaxing young bodies.

GIRLS AND CONTACT SPORTS

When it comes to prepubescent girls, who are physically on a par with or even ahead of boys, the same caveats apply to girls participating in contact or collision sports as are applied to boys. Parents' decision as to whether or not to let their daughters participate in contact sports at this age should be guided by considerations that apply to prepubescent kids regardless of sex. (See also "Contact and Collision Sports," page 16.)

For girls who have already reached puberty, however, opinions are divided about whether or not it is appropriate to participate in such contact-heavy sports as football and ice hockey or in contact sports with boys. Dr. Andrew Price, pediatric orthopedic surgeon at New York University Hospital, explains why he is not a big fan of contact or collision sports for girls: "Girls have less lean body mass than boys. They don't have as much muscle, and muscle is a stabilizer that also has a protective function in terms of injury."

> *"Certain men and women might be a good match in lacrosse and soccer, but the women would have to have strength training."*
> *—Dr. Lyle Micheli, director of the Sports Medicine Division at Children's Hospital, Boston, Mass.*

Ultimately it's up to the child and her parents to come to a decision. If a girl does decide to compete in a contact or collision sport, it is vitally important that she be of equal size, weight and strength as the other youngsters she'll be playing with.

GIVING GIRLS A LIFT — WEIGHT TRAINING

There are various pros and cons concerning weight training for kids (see also "Weight Training," page 89) but there do not seem to be any special caveats for girls:

> *"Weight training can be just as beneficial to girls as to boys. Done with proper guidance, weight training for girls will not develop bulging, unattractive muscles. Rather, young women who use resistive exercises as part of their preparation for athletics will find themselves becoming more lithe and vibrant."*
> *—Dr. Ernie Vandeweghe, pediatrician and former basketball player for the New York Knicks*

NUTRITION FOR GIRLS

Apart from maintaining healthy eating habits there are a few special nutritional concerns for girls.

Certain vitamin and mineral deficiencies, notably deficiencies in calcium and iron — as well as a decrease in bone mineral density — are common among female athletes.

"If you have a young girl in a highly intensive training program, it's important to give her calcium supplements," says Dr. Andrew Price. "If she has decreased bone mineral density, then she is more susceptible to stress fractures and overuse problems. I would give her calcium tablets. Calcium is virtually never harmful, because the body absorbs only so much and excretes the rest."

Before your daughter takes calcium, iron or any other supplements, however, it's advisable to consult a physician.

Part 4
Shaping Up

> "I don't accept it when people tell me that they don't have time to eat. They have the time, but they haven't made the commitment to making the eating of breakfast and lunch the priority that it should be."
> —*Nancy Clark, sports nutritionist at Sportsmedicine-Brookline, Massachusetts, author of* The Sports Nutrition Guidebook

> "Intensive bursts of activity, a natural way of life in childhood, are a child's own way of keeping fit. Conditioning and training before puberty will never show the results one would expect after experience with older subjects."
> — *Dr. Thomas E. Shaffer, College of Medicine, Ohio State University, Columbus, Ohio*

NUTRITION

Good nutrition is important for all kids, but especially for those who are active in sports and who need the energy only a proper balanced diet can provide. It's not just a question of eating right for a particular game or competition; if a child eats a single nutritionally sound meal before a sporting event, it won't make up for dozens of inadequate ones. Performance will usually rely more on the foods and beverages consumed days, and sometimes weeks, prior to an event. By eating healthy foods regularly during childhood, not only do kids get the energy they need, but also they establish eating habits that will contribute to better health later in life.

Daily Diet

There are more than 50 nutrients that a child's body needs on a daily basis—all of which are present in the proverbial well-balanced diet. By "diet," I mean dietary intake, not calorie counting. A kid's diet is simply food: a little bit of this, a little bit of that. According to Dr. Ronald Kleinman, associate chief of the Pediatric Gastro-Intestinal and Nutrition Unit, Massachusetts General Hospital, and chairman of the Academy of Pediatrics Committee on Nutrition, "There isn't enough information at this point to be sure you'll do damage by not paying obsessive attention to [a child's] diet at this age, and a fair amount of information to suggest that children have a wide range of tolerance when there's a variety of foods in the diet."

To ensure variety and a well-rounded diet, dole out moderate portions from the Basic Four Food Groups: 1) meat and fish (including poultry); 2) dairy (milk, eggs and cheese); 3) grains (bread and cereal); and 4) fruits and vegetables.

Water

Water is the most vital nutrient at any age. A child can go weeks without certain vitamins or minerals (although I wouldn't suggest they do so) without ill effects; but without consuming an adequate amount of water, athletic performance can be affected in less than an hour. Losing as little as 2-3% of your body weight via perspiration can cause a decrease in concentration, coordination, strength and stamina. A child's body is 60 - 70% water. If large unreplaced losses of fluid occur, the result can be heat stroke and in extreme cases death.

Water should be consumed in substantial amounts daily—as much as five to eight glasses, depending on the weight of the child. During intense exercise the child should drink even more. Contrary to popular myth kids won't get stomach cramps from drinking reasonable amounts of water before, during and after sports participation. Consuming large amounts of water prior to or during activity should have no adverse effects on performance (other than frequent trips to the bathroom, which might, for some kids, be embarrassing).

Guidelines for the Picky Eater

Here are a few suggestions for making sure even the pickiest eaters get the foods they need:

- Remove all nutrient-poor foods from the house.

- Set an example of good eating habits; don't ask a child to eat anything that you wouldn't eat.

- Offer children two choices for snacks (and meals, if possible), rather than present an unlimited selection.

- Avoid liquids before meals; they might fill a child's small stomach, leaving little room for more nutritious fare.

- Do not bribe, threaten or reward a child with food; if a child will not eat, remove the food without a fuss and offer a nutritious snack

- Eat all meals (and as many snacks as you can) with children; if you can't be with them, leave explicit instructions with the person who's supervising them or prepare ready-to-eat and/or heat-and-serve foods.

- If a food is rejected, introduce it again later. If it's turned down again, try something else with a similar nutritional value.

- Take advantage of children's natural curiosity to encourage trying new foods. Use different color, flavor and texture combinations.

- Make the eating experience pleasant and relaxing.

- Be enthusiastic about food; your interest, if not your precise tastes, will soon be shared by children.

Low-Fat Meals for Kids — Are They a Must?

With today's increased cholesterol consciousness, parents might wonder how early to begin limiting the cholesterol intake of children. The evidence is not all in, but experts do offer some guidelines.

The most important thing to know is that you should never put an infant or young child on a diet of any kind—including a heart-healthy one—without consulting first with a physician.

The American Heart Association has developed a "prudent diet" that is based on the principle of basic food groups, with a few more precise recommendations:

- After age two nonfat milk replaces whole milk.

- Eggs are limited to no more than three per week.

- Fish and skinned poultry are consumed more than fatty cuts of beef, pork and lamb.

- Whole grain breads and cereals, vegetables and fruits are emphasized.

- Sugar, fat and salt are reduced.

Dr. Ernst Wynder, president of the American Health Foundation, advises "low-fat diets for every young person between the ages of 2 and 19 whose total cholesterol measures above 170." He also suggests that

(continued on page 77)

Daily Food Guide/ Checklist for School-Age Kids

Food Group	Required Servings
MILK AND CHEESE	**4**
MEAT GROUP (protein foods)	**3** (more permitted)
Eggs	
Lean meat, fish, poultry, dried beans and peas	
Peanut butter	
FRUITS AND VEGETABLES	**4** (more recommended)
Vitamin C source (citrus fruits, berries, tomato, cabbage, cantaloupe)	**1** (or more)
Vitamin A source (green or yellow fruits and vegetables)	**1** (or more)
Other vegetables (including potato)	**2**
Other fruits (apple, banana)	
CEREALS (whole-grain or enriched)	**4** (more recommended)
Breads, buns	
Ready-to-eat cereals	
Cooked grains (cereals, macaroni, rice)	

(every child be tested for high cholesterol. "Heart attacks do not begin in childhood, but atherosclerosis does."

Dr. Laurence Finberg, chairman of the Department of Pediatrics at the Children's Medical Center of Brooklyn, believes universal testing is excessive. The nutrition committee of the American Academy of Pediatrics—formerly chaired by Finberg—recommends that children from high-risk families "in which a close relative has any sort of atherosclerotic disease or high cholesterol" be tested. To reduce cholesterol levels in kids the Academy suggests a diet that supplies no more than 30% of its calories from fat. (Currently children in the U.S. get about 37% of their calories from fat, just like their parents.)

Up until the age of two, a child needs fats (of which mother's milk has plenty). But low-fat after the age of two, says Dr. Finberg, is fine. "Going from whole milk to two-percent or skim milk won't hurt children over two. And they'll still get the calcium they need." Finberg does not recommend cutting meat entirely from a child's diet; just keep it lean.

Parents should review the evidence themselves, and consult with their pediatrician before altering their children's diet.

Nutrition During Growth Spurts

When prepubertal growth begins — at about eight or nine for girls, and a year or two later for boys — kids start laying down fat deposits that will soon find compensation in height increases. Their appetites are also growing. This is the time to make sure that kids stay on the move — through sports or just playing around. They need to establish healthy, active habits that will continue on after their growth peaks and calorie needs decline.

Dr. Finberg mentions calcium, iron and zinc as the key minerals for growth periods "because they're the hardest to obtain, particularly if you're on a low-fat diet, as they tend to be associated with animal fat." A balanced diet will probably provide kids with sufficient amounts of these minerals. Milk is a great source of calcium; leafy green vegetables such as spinach provide plenty of iron; and zinc can be found in a variety of foods, including seafood, meat, chicken, nuts, eggs, lentils, beans and peas.

Eating On the Run

Eating not just well, but regularly, is the key to good health. Breakfast and lunch, in particular, are the meals that provide a child's body with the calories (and therefore the energy) it needs. Even if parents and kids are running late in the morning and there's no time for a complete breakfast, there's still enough time for orange juice, muffins, fruit or yogurt.

The old adage about breakfast being the most important meal of the day is certainly true for kids. Whatever form the meal takes, it's important for kids to eat early in the day. Studies have shown that when children begin their day without a morning meal, they're less attentive, more irritable and lethargic. This means that they won't have the proper physical and/or mental energy for work or play, and that they will be more prone to making mistakes.

Fast Foods

Nutritionist Nancy Clark recommends some of her favorite no-cook meals and/or quickly-prepared hot dinners: English muffin pizzas, stoned wheat crackers, peanut butter and milk, vegetable soup with extra broccoli and a sprinkling of Parmesan cheese, tuna sandwich with tomato soup, and bran cereal with banana and raisins.

In addition, she keeps these foods ready to go:

- *In the refrigerator:* low-fat cheese, cottage cheese, yogurt, milk, eggs, bananas, carrots, V-8 juice

- *In the freezer:* English muffins, pita bread, multi-grain bread, orange juice concentrate, broccoli, cauliflower, spinach, winter squash, cut-up chicken, extra-lean hamburger, ground turkey patties

- *In the cupboard:* spaghetti, rice, ramen noodles, potatoes, wheat crackers, Ry-Krisp, spaghetti sauce, minced clams, tuna, canned salmon, kidney beans, peanut butter, bran flakes, oat bran, Museli, raisins

Vitamin Supplements

Nutritionists and physicians maintain that a balanced diet provides sufficient nutrients for most children. Vitamin and nutrition supplements and "special" foods for active kids are unnecessary and expensive, and they can be dangerous. Generally speaking, increased activity does not increase the need for any nutrient intake except for energy; this increased requirement for energy can be filled by such foods as complex carbohydrates (see also "Carbo Loading," page 80). The need for certain vitamins does increase during exercise, but this increase is small and can be easily met by the additional food intake required by such exercise.

The only thing a vitamin or mineral will cure is a deficiency of that particular vitamin or mineral. Parents shouldn't take it upon themselves to give their children supplements; doing so can prove dangerous. For instance vitamin A toxicity can result in dry flaky skin, severe headaches, bone and joint pains and liver damage. And mega-doses (those far in excess of the amount absorbed through a normal diet) of niacin, vitamin B6, vitamin C, vitamin D, iron, magnesium, zinc and other vitamins and minerals have also been shown to have some harmful effects.

I would make one exception to this rule: I do believe there is something to the magical cold-fighting properties attributed to vitamin C by such medical health experts as Nobel Prize-winning scientist Linus Pauling (though medical experts are still divided on the issue). A time-released program of Vitamin C—for example, 500 milligrams three times a day—may be helpful, in concert with other recommended remedies, such as plenty of fluids, rest and chicken soup. This is a reasonable nontoxic dose; any excess is flushed through the body, not absorbed.

Salt Tablets

There is no need to take salt tablets — ever. Most kids get sufficient amounts of salt in their regular diet. If for some reason extra salt *is* needed, it can be added to meals or consumed through salty foods such as pizza, nuts, or chips.

Salt loss can be an issue for young athletes, causing the muscles to cramp up. If cramping due to salt loss occurs, consult a physician. Rather than have you run to the pharmacy for salt pills, your doctor will probably recommend potassium-rich foods, such as citrus fruits and juices (grapefruit, banana and orange), as well as potatoes, tomatoes and milk.

Sports Drinks

Advertisements for sports drinks usually claim that they replace electrolytes, which are involved in fluid balance, nerve conduction and muscle contraction. While it is true that electrolytes are lost via sweat during athletic activity, after exercise electrolyte replacement can be achieved with a normal diet. There is no real need for these special drinks. Parents and kids should also be aware that most sports drinks contain sugar, and should therefore not be consumed during activity. Sugar gives an immediate energy "rush," which is usually followed by a "crash." The extreme fluctuation can hinder sports performance.

The body loses a lot more water than electrolytes through exercise. So water replacement is the main concern, and water is the most efficient replacement fluid for kids — before, during or after activity.

Eating Before Game Time

There is no one bill of fare to recommend for kids to consume before a sporting event, but here are a few rules of thumb:

- Game day is not the time to start experimenting with exotic foods. Most kids have enough butterflies floating around in their stomachs; they don't need anything to upset the nest. Baseball star Wade Boggs is known for eating chicken before every game. Though it's probably as much superstition as nutrition, Boggs obviously believes in the powers of poultry. If your kids have a favorite food—providing it's not just empty calories or too filling—let them have a taste.

- Avoid fatty or fried foods, cheese and butter, oil and nuts; these take a long time to digest.

- Avoid processed sugar.

- Keep away from overly filling foods; when coupled with "pregame jitters," they may result in stomach cramps.

- To give the system time to finish digesting a pregame meal, *try to eat about three hours before game time.*

- Drink plenty of water with a pregame meal, especially in hot weather. Another glass of water 90 minutes before game time helps the body's "cooling system." Keep well hydrated before and during competition. It's a myth that drinking too much water during exercise will cause cramps.

- Rather than eating a hefty portion of meat, choose a healthy helping of carbohydrates. A pre-competition meal moderately high in complex carbohydrates (bread, potatoes, rice and pasta are rich in complex carbohydrates) and low in fat is especially recommended for kids participating in "stop-start" sports such as basketball, swimming, football and volleyball.

Carbo Loading

Carbohydrates are the most readily available source of food energy. Glycogen, the major source of energy for working muscles, is manufactured by your body from the carbohydrates you eat. Carbohydrate, or glycogen, loading is a diet-exercise technique that can increase muscle glycogen levels to above normal. For several (usually three to five) days before an event athletes eat a high-carbohydrate diet—consuming as much as 55 – 60 % of total calories as carbohydrates, thereby storing enough glycogen for the needed energy. This diet has been effective for athletes involved in high-endurance sports that require more than 90 minutes of nonstop effort.

For young athletes who don't (and should not) compete at this level, such intensive carbo loading is not advisable. But they could benefit from a light carbo load of five to six grams of carbohydrates per kilogram of body weight. (To convert body weight to kilograms, divide weight in pounds by 2.2.)

Sources of Carbohydrates

Each of the following foods is a good source of carbohydrates:

- bread
- fruit-flavored yogurt
- burritos
- pasta
- tomato juice
- milk
- oatmeal
- chocolate
- pancakes
- raisins
- corn
- asparagus
- carrots
- spinach
- stringbeans
- apples
- oranges

Carbohydrates come in several forms: 1) starches, 2) sugars, or 3) a combination of the two. Starches—including potatoes, pasta, rice, breads and cereals—are excellent sources of *complex carbohydrates,* the "healthy" kind recommended most because they provide a steady release of energy over time. Sucrose (table sugar), the lactose in milk products and the fructose in fruits and juices are called *simple carbohydrates,* which provide more immediate energy. (Natural sugars provide more time-released energy than processed sugars, which give some kids a "sugar rush," an apparent burst of energy, followed by a "crash.") An oatmeal raisin cookie is an example of a mixed carbohydrate, containing both simple and complex carbohydrates.

Sample Menu for Game Day

The portions should vary depending on the child's age and size, and the activity of the day.

On the day of an afternoon game:

BREAKFAST (about 7 a.m.)

- fruit juice and/or fruit—1/2 cup or more
- whole grain, low-sugar cereal—3/4 cup or more
- toast or English muffin—1 or 2 slices topped with
- peanut butter—no more than 2 tablespoons
- egg — 1 or 2; or lean meat (avoid bacon, ham and sausage, which are high in fat) — 1-2 ounces
- low-fat or skim milk—8 ounces
- water—1 or 2 glasses (if desired)

EARLY LUNCH (about 11 A.M., or at least three hours before game time)

- soup (not creamed) — 6-8 ounces
- sandwich (made with whole grain bread, with mustard, not mayonnaise) of turkey or chicken — 1-2 ounces of meat
- fruit—1 cup
- fruit juice and/or low-fat or skim milk—8 ounces
- water—1 or 2 glasses (if desired)

POSTGAME SNACK
   This is optional — to help replenish fluids, minerals and carbohydrates; each of the items should be consumed in reasonable, *not* gargantuan, quantities:

- fruit juice or fruit
- whole grain crackers or bread with cheese or peanut butter
- carrot sticks

> **DINNER**
>
> - fish, poultry or lean meat—3 ounces or more
> - potato, rice or starchy vegetable—1/2 cup or more
> - green or yellow vegetable and/or salad
> - bread—1 slice
> - low-fat or skim milk—8 to 12 ounces
> - water—1 or 2 glasses (if desired)
> - dessert (An oatmeal raisin cookie is preferable to a glazed doughnut, but if the child insists, an occasional taste of "junk food" is O.K. and will be balanced by the rest of the game-day diet.)
>
> *For an evening game:*
> Follow the same basic guidelines—with breakfast and lunch being slightly larger and dinner smaller (served at least three hours before game, with dessert saved as postgame snack).

Obesity

Outside of the huge and ever-present threats of drug, alcohol and tobacco use, obesity is perhaps the central problem facing today's youth. Several studies have confirmed that children are noticeably fatter than they were a generation ago. In the last 20 years the number of obese 12- to 17-year-olds has increased by 39%; in ages 6 – 11, the number has increased by 54%.

For a child it's a doughnut here, a Big Mac there; it only takes an extra 50 to 100 calories a day more than can be expended in physical activity to account for up to 10 additional pounds per year. Baby fat is just that—for babies; when it becomes kid fat, there can be problems. A weight problem during early childhood is usually a harbinger of future battles with obesity. Dr. William Strong, a pediatric cardiologist with the Medical College of Georgia, Augusta, says that "Fast foods have intensified the obesity problem. I don't think there's any problem with having a Taco Bell or McDonald's or any other kind of fast food so long as it's not a routine part of the diet. But these kinds of meals should be eaten no more than once a week. When you are talking about a Big Mac, fries and a strawberry shake, you are talking about 1,100 calories right there. Most adults don't need more than 1,800 to 2,100 calories a day, and here are children with far lower caloric requirements taking that in and then not burning it off."

Admittedly, some portion of obesity can be hereditary (though the actual behavior is often learned). A child born to two obese parents runs an 80% chance of becoming an obese adult, and there's a 40% chance of obesity in families where only one parent is significantly overweight.

Parents should keep in mind that the recommended fat intake of children (and adults) should be about 30% of total daily calories. If your child eats significantly more than that, consult your physician for advice.

EXERCISE

Most kids are so active that it's difficult to get them to stop running and jumping around. Some fitness experts argue that they naturally keep in shape, that a regimen of conditioning exercises is unnecessary for children, that it's superfluous.

Cardiorespiratory fitness, maintains Dr. Shaffer, is usually at a particularly high level during childhood—even without conditioning.

On the other side of the fitness coin there are experts who do recommend an exercise regimen for children. Dr. Roy Shepard of the University of Toronto advocates six to ten minutes of "very vigorous activity each school day." As for long-term fitness, Dr. Shepard suggests that parents encourage youngsters to stay active in more moderate sports such as bicycle riding and roller skating.

Body Benefits

Exercise can help kids with:

1. Blood circulation.
2. Healthy skin.
3. Digestion.
4. Excretion.
5. Heat regulation.
6. Muscle tone.
7. Relieving internal congestion.
8. Strengthening and developing the lungs.
9. Strengthening the heart and muscles.

According to a study conducted by Dr. Charles Linder, a pediatrician at the Medical College of Georgia in Augusta, "habitually active" children are not necessarily any more fit than their more sedentary counterparts, but they do have lower cholesterol levels. "This suggests that you can't get into shape with just a short-term program. It has to be long term," says Dr. Linder.

While there is no consensus on whether or not a fitness regimen in necessary, I'd like to quote from a source who was instrumental in my own physical and mental development: "It couldn't hurt," my Grandma Anna used to say.

Kids and Fitness — a Recent History

In 1943 Dr. Thomas L. Cureton, a professor at the University of Illinois, wrote in the Journal of the American Medicine Association that the physical fitness of American youth was "appalling." A little more than ten years later President Dwight Eisenhower received another failing fitness report card for American children, based on a test administered by renowned fitness expert Bonnie Prudden and her colleague, NYU's Dr. Hans Kraus. They found that of the 4,000 youngsters evaluated, 58% couldn't pass the most basic physical tests.

In the 1960s President John Kennedy strenuously began pushing for fitness in young and old alike, calling the national trend toward softness "a menace to our security as well as our ability to live up to the challenges which lie ahead."

In the 1970s a nationwide preoccupation with fitness took off; everyone seemed to be running, jogging or walking fast. And in the 1980s a septuagenarian president was portrayed as the archetype of clean living and good health.

By all appearances Americans in the 1990s should be the healthiest they have ever been. Surely our young folk are the most fit generation of the modern age.

Not so.

There is an overwhelming number of statistics that seem to disprove the assertion that children are naturally fit. According to the standards set by the President's Council on Physical Fitness and Sports and the National Center for Health Statistics:

- Sixty-four percent of today's children ages 6 – 17 fail to meet basic fitness guidelines.
- Fifty percent of all girls and 25% of all boys can't do a single pull-up; 40% of the boys can only do one pull-up.
- Forty-two percent of all children have high levels of cholesterol.

- Thirty-three percent of all boys 6 to 12—and 50% of girls ages 6 – 17—cannot run a mile faster than walking speed (about 10 minutes).

- Forty percent of children ages 5 – 8 have at least one risk factor for heart disease, including high blood pressure, high cholesterol, obesity or low cardiovascular efficiency.

And there's more:

- According to the federally funded National Children and Youth Fitness Study conducted by health researcher Jim Ross of 8,000 kids ages 10 – 18, only about 50% of the children questioned exercised on a regular basis; only about 33% are enrolled in daily physical education programs in their schools.

- A School Population Fitness Survey of 19,000 public school children ages 6 – 17 found a low level of performance on heart-lung endurance tests, sit-ups, and arm and shoulder muscle strength.

Enough gloom and doom. We have an idea of what the situation is. The question is: What's a poorly conditioned boy or girl to do?

According to the President's Council the prescription for healthier, more physically fit kids can be found in:

- Substantial doses of quality daily physical education (minimum class time of 30 minutes) for all students in kindergarten through 12th grade.

- Major emphasis on lifetime physical fitness activities for the development of strength, endurance and flexibility for health and performance.

- Physical fitness testing at least twice yearly (preferably in the fall and spring).

- Programs designed to accommodate students at all ability levels.

P.E. classes, league sports and general running around will provide most kids with the exercise they need, but parents should be aware of any fitness failings, and be prepared to bring their children's physical fitness up to an acceptable level.

Creating an Exercise Program

Even if kids are active and get sufficient exercise with their daily routine, it's good to start early on a fitness program. They may not need it now, but they certainly will someday. It will give them a jump on the aging process.

When establishing an exercise program for kids, remember to keep it simple and short. You can't expect them to do too much for too long. More than five minutes and most kids will lose interest.

Parents (and/or coaches) should perform the exercises right along with the kids. Have some fun with them; yell out mock commands like a drill sergeant, or come up with your own creative, even goofy-looking, exercises. It stands to reason: If children enjoy an activity, they will look forward to doing it. Any activity that gets kids moving around will probably be good for overall fitness and sports readiness. It might not be a good idea to focus too much on any particular part of the body, but exercises that help build overall flexibility and strength will be beneficial to young athletes.

Flexibility

Most extraordinary athletes move with a kind of grace and fluidity. This seeming effortlessness is usually the result of flexibility.

> *"The flexible athlete is physically more adaptable. He is able to change direction more quickly and easily. There is less chance that he will be injured."*
> *— Dr. Ernie Vandeweghe, pediatrician and former basketball player for the New York Knicks*

Stretching is probably the best way to increase muscle and tissue flexibility. This helps to relieve muscle tension, which in turn facilitates ease of movement, which can result in enhanced athletic performance.

Some kids are born with flexibility, while others have to work harder to develop it. Dr. Vandeweghe suggests that most stretching exercises be performed as follows:

1. *Static:* Avoid bouncing or ballistic motion. The body should be relaxed throughout the stretch, not tense or strained.
2. *Under control:* Avoid sudden movements. Keep all actions deliberate and smooth.
3. *To the end point:* Move to a point where you can feel the muscles stretching, and stop. Hold that point for the allotted time (say, 20 seconds, depending on the exercise), and then slowly return to position.

4. *Individually designed:* Each child should progress at his own rate and adjust the stretching exercises according to his needs.

Seven Stretching Steps for a More Flexible Child

Pediatric orthopedic surgeon Dr. Andrew Price suggests these basic exercises suitable for all ages. Each exercise should be performed twice for 20 to 30 seconds (the younger the child, the lesser duration), without any bouncing in any of the motions:

1. *"Hurdler's Stretch" for quadriceps:* Lie flat on your back with the left leg stretched out straight in front of you and the right leg bent back so that the foot is as close to the right hip as you can get it. Keeping the pelvis down and the lower back pressed into the ground, hold onto the right ankle with the right hand, and try to press the back of the knee to the ground. Repeat with the left leg bent back.

2. *"Hurdler's Stretch" for hamstrings:* Use the same starting position as for the previous stretch, with one leg straight in front of you and the other leg bent back. Raise the upper body so that you're in a seated position, then try to touch the toe of the outstretched leg with both hands. This is a two-parter: first, try to touch the toe, keeping the knee of the outstretched leg straight; this will stretch the hamstrings close to knee. Then bend the outstretched leg slightly, so that the knee raises off the ground a little (but the heel still touches the ground); this will stretch the other end of the muscle. Repeat both stretches with the other leg outstretched.

3. *"Back to Back" for back:* Lie flat on your back with legs stretched out in front of you on the ground. Pull the right knee to chest, keeping the other leg as flat as possible. Repeat with the left leg. Then pull both knees to the chest.

4. *"The Twister" for flank, pelvic girdle, lower back:* Lie flat on the ground with legs out straight and arms stretched out perpendicular to the body. Keeping the shoulders to the ground, raise the right leg straight up in the air, then cross it over to the left side of the body, stretching the gluteals and the flanks. Try to keep both legs as straight as possible. Repeat with the left leg, twisting it over to the right side of the body.

5. *"Heel-Cord Stretch" for heel cord (Achilles tendon):* Stand facing a wall, with one foot in front of you and the other foot

behind you, toes of both feet straight ahead. (You should be standing far enough away from the wall so that when your palms are pressed against it, your arms are stretched out straight). Pushing both palms against the wall, bend the forward leg slightly at the knee, and keep the back leg straight, with the heels of both feet flat on the ground. You should feel the stretch in the back calf and up near your knee. After holding that stretch, slightly bend, or "crack", the knee of the back leg, and hold. This time you should feel the stretch down lower, closer to the ankle. Repeat both stretches with the other leg forward.

6. *"Hip Flexors" for buttocks:* Stand upright in front of a chair or any flat surface that's raised up a foot or two. Stand far enough away from the chair so that when you rest one foot on the chair, the other foot is behind you (not underneath or ahead), and you're "leaning into" the chair. Standing in this position, push the groin forward. You'll feel the stretch in the back of the behind. Repeat with other leg on the chair.

7. *"Toe Raisers" for ankles:* Stand on the edge of a step, so that the balls of the feet rest firmly on the step, with toes pointed in toward each other and heels suspended in air, pointing away from each other. Holding on to a bannister or wall for balance, rise up on the balls of your feet as high as you can, then go back down. Repeat 25 times with toes turned in, then 25 times with toes turned out and heels facing each other, 25 with toes turned in, 25 with toes turned out. Three sets of 25 each will strengthen ankles.

Strength

Strength is an essential component in every athletic activity. Overall strength is usually stressed, although various sports may emphasize certain areas more than other. For example, increased leg strength is beneficial for basketball, running and soccer, while for baseball, football and swimming, upper torso and arm strength are important.

Professional athletes usually build up their strength through some form of weight training.

Weight Training

For years conventional wisdom dictated that prepubescent kids could gain few, if any, benefits from a program of resistance strength exercises; most physicians believed that they could be harmful. The opposition to strength training for prepubescent children had been

> ### Running Around
>
> According to Dr. Ernie Vandeweghe, "Running is such a natural activity that most of us never stop to see if we are doing it right." So to make sure you're making the most of your runs, try to follow these tips:
>
> 1. Relax. The body does its best work when it's supple.
>
> 2. Develop proper stride. Again, free and easy works best. The average stride is about a body length.
>
> 3. Lean forward. Body angle is important. You should be angled slightly forward with your head up, and your ankles, hips and shoulders in a straight line.
>
> 4. Don't bend forward. Lean, don't bend. Bending from the waist can slow a runner down.
>
> 5. Maintain good arm action. Again, keep both arms relaxed so they don't become heavy. They should be held so the angle between the upper and lower arm forms a little less than a 90-degree angle. Arms should be brought forward in a pumping motion, with the hands moving toward the center of the body. As arms come back they should never pass beyond hips.

based on three basic beliefs: 1) these kids lack the necessary hormones for significant strength gains; 2) such gains, if attainable, would not benefit performance or reduce the risk of injury in children's sports; and 3) resistive weight training is dangerous for kids, with an unacceptable risk of injury.

Only recently has this type of strength-building program been considered for children. In a study of 10- and 11-year-old prepubescent children, Les Sewall and Dr. Lyle Micheli of the Sports Medicine Division at Boston's Children's Hospital, found that kids who undertook a program of weight training showed a 40% increase in strength without incurring any injuries (compared to a 10% gain among kids who didn't participate in weight training). "Providing the program is well supervised," Sewell and Micheli conclude, "all the movements are done in slow controlled motions and excessive weights are avoided, resistance training can benefit prepubescent children."

Many in the medical community admit that their resistance has been somewhat modified by the study. Says Dr. Andrew Price, pediatric orthopedic surgeon, New York University Hospital, "I would never have recommended weight training for kids before puberty. But after looking at this study, I think that, in certain instances—specifically, for rehabilitation of an injury—weight training can be beneficial."

Developing a Weight Training Program

AGES	9-11	12-14
Exercises per body part	1	1
Sets	2	3
Repetitions	12-15	10-12
Maximum weight	Very light	Light

There is no single age that is deemed acceptable or advisable to begin weight training, but most of the benefits will be lost on kids younger than 8 or 9. However in some cases, particularly among older children, it has been shown that weight training can reduce the risk of injury by strengthening muscles, tendons and ligaments, thereby making these "structures" more solid.

At any age weight training safety is based on proper technique, and a weight training instructor's initial objective should be to teach the correct technique for each exercise. Improper technique is not only wasted—the muscles are not exercised to the best advantage—but it can also lead to injuries. That's why *a qualified instructor or an experienced spotter should always be present during the child's weight training routine.*

For prepubescent kids, machines (such as Universal, Nautilus, etc.) are considered safer than free weights (barbells, dumbbells, etc.) because the likelihood of a machine weight falling on someone is minimal. Using either method requires supervision, but with free weights, increased vigilance is needed.

Nonweight Resistance Training

Kids can also build strength using "nonweight" resistance training. Several new pieces of equipment using air and water, rather than free weights, to supply resistance are currently on the market. Even the inner tube from an old bicycle tire can be used as a nonweight resistance device by stretching it with the arms or legs (though be careful that the tube doesn't snap). A little creativity can go a long way. There are many different possibilities for nonweight resistance training. But remember, as in weight resistance training, kids who engage in nonweight resistance training should consult a qualified instructor on a proper, effective regimen. In addition, an adult should always be present as a "spotter."

The Physically Underdeveloped Child

One out of six children in the United States is characterized by the President's Council on Physical Fitness and Sports as physically "underdeveloped." Underdeveloped kids, or those "who fall below minimum acceptable standards for strength and endurance," have a more serious problem than just being out of shape. Therefore it is extremely important to identify these kids and ensure that they receive proper help.

The President's Council has developed a screening test designed to identify those young people. The test measures 1) arm/shoulder strength and endurance, 2) abdominal strength and endurance, and 3) circulatory/respiratory and muscular endurance. Parents, coaches and teachers should look for these obvious "danger" signals:

- Breathlessness that persists long after exercise

- Blueness of lips that is not due to cold or dampness

- Pale, clammy skin or cold sweating during or after exercise

- Unusual fatigue

- Persistent shakiness after exercise

- Muscle twitching

Parents in particular should be mindful of these additional warning signs that may not be as easily discernible to a teacher or coach:

- Headaches

- Dizziness

- Fainting

- Broken sleep

- Digestive upset

- Pain not associated with injury

- Uneven heartbeat or severe pounding of the heart

- Disorientation or personality changes

If you think your child might be physically underdeveloped, don't automatically put him on a strenuous exercise regimen. Go to a doctor to confirm your findings, and ask his advice in coordinating an appropriate fitness regimen with the P.E. instructor or other sports professional.

Part 5
Injury Prevention and Treatment

WARNING: This section should not be used as a diagnostic tool, nor as a substitute for a visit to a physician. The purpose of presenting this material is to give parents more information about their children's bodies, so they can ask their doctors more pointed and pertinent questions.

Most children will engage in sports without ever being seriously injured. But not all. Thankfully, most children's sports injuries are minor, requiring less than seven days' restricted activity (including injuries sustained in organized football leagues). The majority consist of contusions, sprains and strains, mainly to the knee and ankle; only 6 – 8 % of all injuries are fractures.

Pediatric orthopedic surgeon Dr. Andrew Price says, "Seeing the injuries enumerated by sport in black and white might cause some increased trepidation with parents. If, for example, there is mention of head and neck injuries in hockey, a parent may immediately fantasize about the most terrible spine-severing injury imaginable. It's just not the case. Your child has more chance of injuring himself in a drive with you—though I'm not disparaging anyone's driving skills—than in a supervised game of non-contact ice hockey. Overall, the injury rate of kids in sports is quite low; and parents should keep that in perspective."

The first and most important rule for injury prevention and treatment is this: Never push kids when they're injured. Don't tell them to "play through pain." Don't tell them to "shake it off and get out there." And don't tell them, "Big kids don't cry."

That said, what immediately follows is a brief glossary of sports-related injuries, along with equally brief descriptions of treatment where relevant — a sort of pocket diagnostic. But again: Two sentences of treatment tips cannot compare with the 12 years of medical training received by physicians. When a child is injured—unless the injury is so minor that it can be adequately addressed on site—parents should remove their child from sports activity until a physician has been consulted.

GLOSSARY OF SPORTS INJURIES

Abrasion: An injury that scrapes off the outer skin and exposes underlying tissue. Clean the wounded area with soap and water, and apply a soothing antibiotic ointment to prevent infection.

Contusion: Internal bleeding, usually followed by swelling, caused by a direct blow against the skin. Apply cold compresses and a pressure bandage immediately. After the swelling subsides, apply heat locally. Insist on rest until the bleeding is controlled.

Dislocation: The displacement of the opposing continuous surfaces of bone making up a joint, resulting in gross deformity of the joint, and severe pain. No one who is not professionally qualified should attempt to replace the dislocated bone. See an orthopedist immediately for expert attention. Do not resume activity after the dislocated bone is put back into place.

Fracture: There are several types of fractures; all should be immediately X-rayed. *Simple fracture:* the bone, but not the skin, breaks. *Compound fracture:* the bone and the skin break (bone may even protrude through skin). *Impacted fracture:* the bone breaks and the broken ends of the bone are jammed together. *Green-stick fracture:* the bone is cracked, but doesn't break off completely. (Stress fractures are discussed separately, below.)

Hematoma: Blood collects in tissues (usually visible under the skin), generally as a result of a blow to the body. Apply an ice pack and pressure dressing to stem bleeding.

Laceration: A wound caused by a sharp object, in which the skin is cut through its full thickness. Seek medical help for cleaning and bandaging. Stitches are often required.

Macrotrauma (acute injury): A sudden, serious one-shot episode where something breaks, snaps or tears. Seek medical help immediately.

Microtrauma (overuse syndrome): An injury that develops over time, such as a stress fracture. May need X-ray or bone scan to identify. Seek medical help.

Fractures Tell Tales

Dr. Ernie Vandeweghe, pediatrician and former New York Knick, cites several warning signs that could indicate a fracture:

1. A "click" heard by athlete, coming from the injured part of body.

2. Tenderness and swelling at the point of injury.

3. Grating of the bone.

4. Sudden stabbing pain on movement.

5. Muscle spasms or hard contractions in the injured area.

6. Deformity of the injured area.

7. Athlete's awareness that something is wrong: If a child complains, listen.

Muscle Spasm or Cramping: Spasms and cramping are caused by a change in the amount of blood fed to the muscle, or by a lack of salt in the blood system. Firmly but smoothly rub the area around the affected muscle—no pounding or too-hard rubbing. Warm (but not hot) compresses and gentle stretching will help alleviate the condition.

Osteochondritis Dissecans: A segment of "dead bone" adjacent to a joint, caused by an interruption of the blood supply to the segment. Circumstances causing the condition are not always clear, but the knee is most commonly affected. A cast is often recommended if growth plates are open; surgery is occasionally an option.

Puncture: A wound made by a blunt object that pierces through the layers of the skin. Check damaged area and penetrating object to make sure that no part of the object is left inside the wound. Seek immediate medical attention; stitches are not always required.

Spondylolysis: A relatively common stress fracture in the lower part of the spine caused by fatigue loading, overuse and/or the repetition of certain movements stressful to the lower back. Seek medical attention; sometimes limitations to training and motion are recommended.

Sprain: An injury to a ligament. There are three basic types of sprains: 1) mild sprain is usually accompanied by slight internal bleeding (apply an Ace bandage); 2) moderate sprain entails some degree of functional loss (protection of the sprained area is essential to the healing process — seek a physician's advice); and 3) severe sprain results in complete functional loss (surgery is often needed — immediate medical attention is required). (See also "Sprains and Strains," page 101.)

Strain: Damage to a tendon or muscle due to overuse or overstress. An ordinary strain, with minor swelling and tenderness, should be rested for a few days; there is usually little damage. For a serious strain, where the muscle or tendon is torn or ruptured, medical attention is needed. (See also "Sprains and Strains," page 101.)

Stress fractures: Micro-fractures that result from overuse, rather than a macrotrauma. Symptoms include local tenderness around bone, pain related to activity, and sometimes swelling. A standard X-ray does not always show the fracture initially; often the way to diagnose stress fracture is by a bone scan, which will reveal the affected area.

SPECIFIC YOUTH INJURIES

Here is a more in-depth look at a few of the more common kids' sports injuries:

Little League Elbow

This is an overuse syndrome that occurs over time, not an acute trauma that happens suddenly. In most cases of this syndrome the medial collateral ligament, on the inside of the elbow, becomes chronically stressed and inflamed as a result of stress on the elbow from the acceleration phase of throwing — when the ball is released, after the wind-up but before deceleration.

There is some controversy as to how and why certain kids develop Little League Elbow (which is different from Tennis Elbow, a strain on the *outside* of the elbow). Some experts blame parents for pushing their kids too hard at too young an age, for all those years of forcing kids to throw with underdeveloped muscles. Some blame coaches for teaching and encouraging prepubescent kids to throw a curveball, which involves an unnatural motion that puts additional strain on the medial collateral ligament. Recent medical evidence points to the repetition and overuse in the throwing motion—rather than the curveball specifically—as the chief culprit of this condition.

My purely unscientific, common-sense opinion is that throwing a curve at too young an age can come back to haunt — and harm — a child. The motion itself is unnatural; it is not usually performed with the same fluidity as when a fastball is thrown, and should probably not be attempted until the child matures physically.

Symptoms:

- Tenderness along the inside of the elbow.

- Limited motion; inability to extend or flex the arm.

- Pain, particularly during throwing activities.

Treatment:

- Rest. The elbow rarely needs to be immobilized, although a splint may be used if the elbow is acutely painful.

- Avoid all throwing activities or painful situations.

- Review the mechanics of throwing and rectify any improper technique.

- Once the inflammation subsides, begin a physical therapy program to regain any motion and strength that might have been lost during the period of inactivity.

- When there is a full range of motion without any pain, get *gently* back into throwing (with the proper mechanics). If the child is a pitcher, she shouldn't pitch more than three innings per game, or more than six innings per week. (In Little League baseball, this three-inning rule was instituted to prevent overuse injuries such as Little League Elbow.)

Osgood-Schlatters Disease

Osgood-Schlatters Disease, or a bump on the front of the shinbone, is one of the most common childhood sports-related injuries. An overuse syndrome, it generally occurs at around ages 10 – 13, during the adolescent growth spurt, when young bodies are particularly vulnerable to the pressures generated by the jumping and running they do every day. All this tension can create a microfracture on the upper end of the shinbone, which becomes inflamed. (Because the fractures are so small, they don't always show up on an X-ray.)

Symptoms:

- Tenderness in the injured area.

- Pain in the injured area upon running, jumping, going up stairs, or even kneeling. The severity of pain is highly variable; some kids can barely walk.

Treatment:

- For less severe cases athletic activities must be modified: no running, jumping, or sports of any kind for a period of time.

- For kids who can hardly walk, legs must be immobilized, sometimes in a cast. Surgery is virtually never performed, even in the most severe cases.

- When inflammation is reduced, begin a physical therapy program to stretch and strengthen muscles. The length of treatment will vary; some kids can be cured with simple stretching exercises in a week's time, while for others it might take months or even a year before they can feel 100% again.

- Osgood Schlatters Disease is a "self-limiting" problem, which means that the condition will go away in time, as the growth plate begins to mature. Regardless of the severity of the condition, however, most kids can return to activity levels a lot sooner with physical therapy.

Sever's Disease

This is an overuse syndrome that occurs on the heelbone, usually among kids around ages 8 – 11. It is similar to Osgood-Schlatters, except that tension generated by kids' normal exercise affects the heelbone rather than the shinbone.

Symptoms:

- Tenderness in the injured area.

- Heel often hurts when child rises up on the ball of the foot.

- Tight heel cord.

- In two-thirds of cases, both heels are affected.

Treatment:

- Initially, modification and/or reduction of athletic activity.

- Heel cord stretching exercises.

- Improved or more appropriate footwear (wearing cushion-soled shoes or sneakers, for instance). It's sometimes discovered that kids have been using improper footwear for a particular sport or playing surface—for example, wearing metal spikes on a hard-packed dirt playing field.

Growth-plate Injuries

As mentioned earlier (see also "Open Growth Plates," page 5), growth plates are the soft cartilage in kids' bones that is responsible for bone growth. In children open growth plates are often the weakest link, making the bones more prone to fracture. From birth until about age 13, the growth plates are weak, although kids are more prone to different types of growth-plate-related injuries at different times:

From about *ages 6 – 10*, bones are vulnerable to macrotrauma. At *ages 6 – 8*, open growth plates around the knee in particular make these kids more susceptible to a bone injury there; a fracture through the growth plate at this age can cause severe leg-length discrepancy and angular deformities. At *ages 10 – 12*, because of the adolescent growth spurt, muscle injuries may be more common; the bones are growing at a fast rate, but the surrounding muscles and ligaments are lagging behind, resulting in decreased flexibility and strength, particularly around the knee. At *12 – 13*, when the growth plates are just about to close, a fracture through the growth plate is rarely as serious. Symptoms and treatment will vary, depending upon the specific injury.

Back Injuries

Back pain is relatively uncommon in children. Even children with scoliosis (curvature of the spine) do not usually experience pain. So if a child complains of back pain, it's important to investigate thoroughly; it could be a sign of a fracture, infection or even a tumor.

X-rays should be taken, and if nothing unusual shows up there, then a bone scan should be done. A negative bone scan will virtually rule out the presence of anything serious.

Sprains and Strains

These are among the most common injuries to befall the young athlete, and as such they deserve more complete mention than is provided in the "Glossary of Sports Injuries," page 98.

The American Medical Association (AMA) classifies strains and sprains in three categories:

Grade I (minor): No appreciable disruption of tissue and a minimal loss of function; this type of injury heals by primary repair, and can be managed by most pediatricians. Minor injuries can be painful, but the pain usually subsides after a short time (though it may recur later or the following day). A child who can run off the field unassisted probably has sustained a minor injury.

Grade II (moderate): Some disruption of tissue (ligament or muscle/tendon) and a partial loss of function; healing usually occurs with primary repair; the potential for scar formation exists. Pediatricians who specialize in sports injuries can manage these injuries, though an orthopedist should probably be consulted.

Grade III (severe): Significant or complete disruption of tissue with a marked or complete loss of function; healing is accompanied by scar formation; requires care of an orthopedist. Severe injuries tend to involve sustained intense pain, especially with movement; they usually call for an immediate cessation of activities.

Children generally sustain minor injuries because they do not generate high-impact force, even in contact sports (unless, of course, one child is appreciably larger and faster than another). Grade III injuries usually occur in extraordinary situations: If the velocity at impact has been augmented by a bike or skateboard; or if there is an immoveable non-giving surface, such as a concrete block or a tree.

For treatment, the following is recommended:

Grade I:

- The initial objective is to relieve pain, spasm and swelling. For the first 24 hours use traditional RICE therapy, which consists of 1) Rest (cessation of activity); 2) Ice (applied for 30 minutes, four times a day, for three days); 3) Compression (Ace bandage); and 4) Elevation.

- For the second 24 hours start rehabilitation but continue steps 2, 3 and 4 above.

- For the third 24 hours continue rehabilitation (depending on injury, it may or may not be advisable to start weight-bearing), and steps 2 and 3 of RICE therapy.

- Beyond 72 hours treatments vary. Contrast therapy (alternating hot with cold) may sometimes be used.

(Generally, heat has no place in treating contusions.)

Grade II:

- The primary goal is the protection of the injured area so that primary healing can proceed. As with Grade I injuries, immediate RICE therapy is recommended. In addition, analgesics and anti-inflammatory agents may be prescribed.

- A significant period of protective immobilization. This may require crutches, taping, splinting or casting. The length of immobilization varies; depending on the amount of tissue damage, it can be as long as six to ten weeks.

- A program of rehabilitation. During the period of immobilization, strength may decrease as much as 1% per day, and aerobic power can be reduced between 10% and 25%. Subsequent rehabilitation is obviously critical in order for the child to regain strength and endurance.

Grade III:

For Grade III strains and sprains, it's very important that the ligament heal in the physiologically correct position.

- A period of immobilization is a given with virtually all severe injuries. As with Grade II injuries, this may entail the use of crutches, taping, splinting or casting.

- A program of rehabilitation is of paramount importance in helping to regain normal use of the affected area.

Hand Injuries

Kids are prone to constant minor hand and finger injuries, including jammed fingers (fingers with sprained ligaments), mallet fingers (fingers with fractures or ruptured tendons) and other fractures. Luckily if a child injures the same finger several times at a young age, she is not necessarily susceptible to reinjury (unlike adults, who may become susceptible to constant reinjury).

Contributing Factors

Notwithstanding the increased susceptibility to growth plate injuries at an early age, *the likelihood of most sports-related injuries increases as the child grows older*. This is due to 1) increased body size and speed and 2) greater intensity and increased magnitude of competition.

THE SIX "S"s OF INJURY PREVENTION

Properly fitting equipment (including footwear), proper playing surfaces, proper conditioning, proper medical advice, proper strength and flexibility all contribute to a program of injury prevention. Dr. Carl Stanitski, clinical associate professor of orthopedic surgery at the University of Pittsburgh School of Medicine, suggests that there are six predominant factors that can cause injuries, overuse injuries in particular:

1. *Shoes (and other equipment):* Ill-fitting shoes, etc., which can cause repetitive stress.
2. *Surfaces:* Excessively hard, unpadded gym floors; poorly maintained fields.
3. *Speed ("too much, too soon"):* Rushing kids before they're properly conditioned or trained.
4. *Structure (of the body):* Orthopedic mal-alignments, primarily knees and ankles.
5. *Strength:* Inequity between strength and size.
6. *Stretching:* Decrease in flexibility, particularly during rapid adolescent growth spurt.

VISITING A PHYSICIAN

If it is decided either by a parent or in a phone consultation with a physician that a child should be taken to a doctor, the visit should usually be made immediately.

During the exam the child should be made as comfortable as possible. Particularly with children, a bedside manner is very important. If the doctor is competent but has a terrible personality, the child could be additionally traumatized by each visit and probably won't cooperate in the treatment. The doctor should tell the child and parents what to expect in the exam, and whether any part of it will be uncomfortable or even painful. There should be no surprises.

Parents and kids should not be afraid to ask questions. Any physician who finds these discussions impertinent or unnecessary is not the doctor for you or your child.

Consulting Kids on Treatment

A lot of decisions reached in sports medicine depend on the specific goals and expectations of the athlete. Every physician should ask each patient, even a child: "What do you want to be able to do?" and then listen to the patient's answer.

Parents, too, have a responsibility to know what their children want. Whether it's a question of surgery, physical therapy or any other type of treatment, make sure you are aware of all the options, and that you discuss them with your child before making a decision.

REHABILITATION AND PHYSICAL THERAPY

Typically, many parents, coaches and doctors assume that most kids can automatically rehabilitate themselves because they're young, flexible and energetic. There is, of course, some factual basis to that belief. However with today's more competitive sports and more intense activities, it's a good idea to set up a directed program of rehabilitation. This provides added protection against future injuries or reinjuries.

The immobilization that is often necessary to proper healing of injuries usually results in stiffness and atrophy of the injured area. Without some sort of physical therapy to bring the injured area up to its previous level of strength and flexibility, the weakened area is more susceptible to reinjury. Physical therapy not only can help kids regain their previous levels of fitness, but in some cases it can make the injured area even stronger than it was before.

Physical therapy should always be conducted under the direction of a professional. For optimum effectiveness it's best to receive therapy directly with the physical therapist in her office. If for whatever reasons it's not feasible to make regular visits to the physical therapist's office, be sure to find out what exercises can be done at home, and make sure a physical therapist instructs you first-hand on proper execution of each exercise.

When to Play, and When Not to Play?

These questions come up frequently. The child comes to the doctor and says, "I have a Little League game this weekend." Or the parent says, "My kid is supposed to go to tennis camp tomorrow and I've already paid for it."

"I can't tell you how many times I have to say to the parents, 'This one sports season is not critical to his entire life.' Or I say to the kid, even though he may hate me for it, 'No, you can't play this week in the big game.' It's just not that important to [warrant risking] permanent injury."
— **Dr. Andrew Price, pediatric orthopedic surgeon, New York University Hospital**

Kids — and parents — must realize that there will always be another game, or another season. When dealing with children's injuries, it's always best to opt for the conservative approach. It cannot be overemphasized that kids should not be taught to play through pain.

INJURIES IN CONTACT SPORTS

There's a lot of concern about the possibility of injury in contact sports. Again, parents and kids should decide for themselves where they stand on the issue of contact. Here are a few statistics that might figure into any parental evaluation:

- Most injuries sustained in organized football leagues require less than seven days' restricted activity.

- A study of six New England Pop Warner football leagues (for kids ages 8–15) revealed a 5% overall rate of significant injury, with fewer than 40% of those injuries categorized as major; no catastrophic injuries occurred. The upper extremities were most likely to be injured, with fractures being the most common type of injury. There was found to be an increased risk of injury in the higher age divisions, due to the greater weight, speed and involvement in "contact activities" of the older kids.

- In a recent study of injury rates in pee wee hockey leagues (approximately ages 12–13), it was found that six times more fractures (or 88% of all fractures) occurred in the leagues that allowed body checking.

DRUG TREATMENT SHOTS

Pills or injections can often mask pain, which can in turn inhibit proper treatment or even exacerbate an injury. Steroid injections can be beneficial for adults in some instances, but shooting cortisone, for example, into a young child's tendon is almost never recommended. "Injecting steroids in tendons will weaken them significantly," says Dr. Andrew Price. "It's particularly crazy for young, active children who're running around a lot. There is an increased risk of rupturing tendons and doing permanent harm.... If parents came to me and said that their kid had a big game and needed to be shot up, I'd tell them to find another doctor."

Parents might want to keep in mind that pain is an indicator that should be respected, not dulled or masked with drugs. And as long as it's not excessive, the level of pain during recuperation and rehabilitation can be an indication of the healing process.

BURNOUT

Years of mental and/or physical strain and pressure associated with sports can lead to burnout. Tennis, gymnastics and swimming have a large number of teenage stars; as such, there is probably more burnout in those sports. Kids' bodies may simply not be up to the intensive training involved.

In tennis, for instance, there's no time limit on a match. A long match can overburden a young athlete's body. But tennis shouldn't be singled out as a culprit; any sport, if allowed to rage out of control, can produce the incendiary mix for burnout.

Bob Wischnia, an editor at *Runner's World*, points to middle-distance running champion Mary Decker Slaney as the prime example of too much, too young: "She was breaking age group records at 10. But she's had more injuries, more stress fractures and surgeries than most runners have. I don't know if you can attribute that all to the insane amount of running she did as a kid, but I think it's a logical conclusion."

Dr. Gabe Merkin, author of several sports medicine books, and once an advocate of road racing for kids, has reversed direction on that opinion. "I now believe it's crazy," he says. "My own son held nine age-group records by the time he was 11. He never ran again."

Parents should look for the symptoms of burnout: withdrawal, fatigue, boredom and overuse injuries. If you see any of these signs in your child, put a limit on the number of hours spent in training and/or competition, and on particularly strenuous movements. (Be sure to do this in conjunction with a doctor.) And even more important, help reduce some of the stress these kids are experiencing by encouraging them to develop a more well-rounded life (see also "Sports Single-mindedness," page 14).

Part 6
A Sport-by-Sport Guide

The following rundown includes information that is relevant to kids' competitive sports and answers basic questions that parents might have regarding possible injuries, equipment, money and time. Not all sports fit into the format; however, some general information is provided for these as well. To find out more about the particulars of each sport — whether or not there is a league or an organization near you — check the list of resources and associations in Part 7.

BASEBALL

Baseball is, relatively speaking, an injury-free sport. Little League Elbow is the most predominant injury. In years past there were many ankle sprains and fractures from sliding into bases, but now "breakaway" bases help avoid those problems. There may be some minimal risk of hand injuries — jammed and mallet fingers, in particular — and possible fractures among kids who slide head first. Helmets are mandatory while batting, and should also be worn while running the basepaths. Catcher's equipment, particularly the mask, should be properly fitted for the individual child. Most youth leagues have banned metal spikes; if they haven't, they should. Batting gloves, which have become increasingly popular for style, can prevent calluses.

Equipment: Most youth leagues provide helmets, bats, balls and catcher's equipment. Parents are expected to buy their kids' footwear (sneakers or cleats) and jockstraps (or protective cups for catchers); they may also decide to outfit their kids with a helmet (if those available do not fit just right) and perhaps a bat.

Season: Most leagues begin play around mid-April and continue through mid- to late June; the season may be extended to make up for rainouts and, of course, for post-season playoffs.

Games: At the younger levels kids usually play about 10 or 12 games per season; older kids may play up to about 18 games per season.

Practice: There is usually a minimum of one practice session a week, lasting at least an hour; again, older kids — because of their longer attention spans — may practice 1 1/2 to 2 hours at each session. If teams are playing only one game per week or if there is an off week in the schedule, coaches might call for two practices in a week.

Fees: Parents may pay from $40 up to $100 (depending on league level and location) for league registration fees; these usually include uniforms, insurance, etc.

For more information:

Coaching Kids to Play Baseball and Softball; by Kurt Aschermann and Gerard P. O'Shea; A Fireside Book—Simon & Schuster; New York; 1985.

Coaching Kids Teeball; by Mike Daney; American Youth Sports; Newhall, Calif.; 1985.

The Father and Son Baseball Book; by Howard Liss; Harper & Row; New York; 1969.

Little League Drills and Strategies; by Ned McIntosh; Contemporary Books; Chicago; 1987.

The Little League Game: How Kids, Coaches and Parents Really Play It; by Lewis Yablonsky and Jonathan Brower; Times Books; New York; 1979.

The Official Little League Fitness Guide; by Frank W. Jobe, M.D., and Diane Moynes, R.P.T.; Simon and Schuster; New York; 1984.

With the Boys: Little League Baseball and Preadolescent Culture; by Gary Alan Fine; University of Chicago Press; Chicago; 1987.

Sports Illustrated Book of Baseball; by the editors of *Sports Illustrated;* Lippincott; Philadelphia; 1966.

BASKETBALL

Basketball is fast becoming as much a contact sport as football, and as such it has its danger quotient. Kids should be cautioned against emulating the pros — particularly by flailing their elbows after a rebound. There are usually a lot of ankle injuries associated with the sport, and conditioning should include exercises to strengthen the ankle. Good high-top sneakers are an essential piece of equipment. There are also a lot of hand and finger injuries — mallet fingers, sprained ligaments and fractures.

Equipment: Balls and, usually, uniforms are supplied by school teams; in local youth (club, church or synogogue) leagues, uniforms are usually an additional expense. Parents are always responsible for outfitting their kids with — when appropriate — sneakers ($25 to $30), jockstraps and protective goggles.

Season: Usually begins around Thanksgiving or early December and may go until the end of March or April.

Games: With so many different types of leagues, it's difficult to generalize. In the New York City school system, for example, middle schools compete interscholastically in about 15 games per regular season.

Practice: Ranges from one hour per week to about six hours per week.

Fees: In interscholastic play there are usually no additional fees; the schools themselves pay for officials, etc. In local leagues there can be a great disparity in costs — again, depending on level and location.

For more information:

Basketball; by Shan Finney; Franklin Watts; New York; 1982.

Basketball Talk for Beginners; by Howard Liss; J. Messner; New York; 1970.

Better Basketball for Boys; by George Sullivan; Dodd, Mead; New York; 1980.

Better Basketball for Girls; by George Sullivan; Dodd, Mead; New York; 1978.

Center; by George Sullivan; T.Y. Crowell; New York; 1988.

Make the Team: Basketball; by Richard J. Brenner; *Sports Illustrated For Kids* Books; 1990.

Sports Illustrated Basketball: The Keys to Excellence; by Neil D. Isaacs and Dick Motta; New American Library; New York; 1988.

BICYCLING

Bicycling is an individual sport that lends itself to lifelong enjoyment. Generally kids sustain very few overuse injuries. Rather the danger of severe injury comes from collisions or falls. It's important that bikes be the correct size and that kids wear a helmet at all times.

There are several different types of cycle-related activities, including mountain biking, off-road biking and simple recreational cycling. Competitively, there is road racing (such as the Tour de France) and BMX (bicycle motocross). The former is not recommended for young kids; the latter is if the kids take proper safety precautions.

Equipment: A bike and a helmet are the two essential pieces of equipment. How much you spend on a bike depends on the type of riding to be done. A good second-hand bike can fill the bill for local paved-street riding, while a pricey mountain bike is more suitable to... well, the mountains. Helmets should be fitted to the individual child and cost anywhere from $25 to $50. Optional accessories include all manner of bicycle clothing and paraphernalia, much of which is not really needed.

For more information:

Better Bicycling for Boys and Girls; by George Sullivan; Dodd, Mead; New York; 1984.

Bicycles Are Fun to Ride; by Dorothy Chlad; Children's Press; Chicago; 1984.

Bicycling Basics; by Tim and Glenda Wilhelm; Prentice-Hall; Englewood Cliffs, N.J.; 1982.

Bikes; by Anne F. Rockwell; Dutton; New York; 1987.

Driving Your Bike Safely; by Corinne J. Naden; J. Messner; New York; 1979.

Wheels! The Kids' Bike Book; by Megan Stine; *Sports Illustrated For Kids* Books; New York; 1990

FIELD HOCKEY

Field hockey is historically a girls' sport (at least in the United States). Though the rules say otherwise, field hockey is a contact sport. For the most part, injuries sustained during participation include contusions, sprains and strains; occasionally there are fractures.

Equipment: A stick, ball, mouthpiece and shin guards are essential; protective goggles for the eyes are optional. Since field hockey's popularity varies around the country, it may be difficult to find all of this equipment at sporting-goods stores. However, the U.S. Field Hockey Association, the sport's national governing body, makes equipment available for about $12 through the local programs it runs.

Season: When played at school, field hockey is a fall sport. Junior field hockey, more often played in community programs, is played in the spring and summer.

Games: Most junior hockey programs tend to stress skills and the fun of playing rather than competition. They even play games without a goalie! The point is that it is *good* for kids to score. Practice sessions can, however, culminate in a scrimmage that simulates game situations.

Practice: Depends on the program. Two-week programs might involve five practice sessions per week; three-month programs would involve two. Practice sessions are generally one or two hours long.

Fees: Local programs sometimes require nominal per-child charges to cover insurance.

For more information:

Basic Field Hockey Strategy; by Lee Ann Williams; Doubleday; Garden City, N.Y.; 1978.

Better Field Hockey for Girls; by George Sullivan; Dodd, Mead; New York; 1981.

Field Hockey is for Me; by Susan Preston-Mauks; Lerner Publications; Minneapolis; 1983.

FOOTBALL

Football is a collision sport with a relatively high number of injuries. There are plenty of contusions and ankle sprains; knee and ankle fractures are common. There is also a greater risk of growth-plate fractures than in any other sport. Parents should be very careful that their children are well matched to the other kids on the team in terms of size, weight and maturity. Proper equipment is vitally important. According to former pro football player Pat McInally: "The face mask should be secure, the chin strap properly fastened and the ear pads placed for tight, firm fit. The shell of the helmet should always be checked for cracks or structural damage." When it comes to football, the more padding the better; kids should make sure all guards (there are usually hip and thigh guards) are secure. Wearing a mouthpiece is also recommended.

Equipment: Parents are expected to buy their kids' footwear (cleats; sneakers are not recommended), mouthpiece and jockstraps (or protective cups). Since helmets must meet very specific requirements in terms of materials and fit, these are almost always provided by the league.

Season: Roughly August 1 through Thanksgiving.

Games: About 10 per season.

Practice: About $1^1/_2$ hours per session; five sessions per week until school starts; three once the school year begins.

Fees: Depends on the locale, but sign-up fees run from $5 to $35.

For more information:

Basic Football Strategy; by Edward F. Dolan; Doubleday; Garden City, N.Y.; 1976.

Be a Winner in Football; by Charles Ira Coombs; Morrow; New York; 1974.

Better Football for Boys; by George Sullivan; Dodd, Mead; New York; 1980.

The First Book of Football; by John Madden; Crown Publishers; New York; 1988.

Football for Young Champions; by Robert Joseph Antonacci; McGraw-Hill; New York; 1976.

Football is for Me; by Lowell A. Dickmeyer; Lerner Publications; Minneapolis; 1979.

Power Basics of Football; by James Bryce and Bill Polick; Prentice-Hall; Englewood Cliffs, N.J.; 1985.

Sports Illustrated Football: Winning Offense; by Bud Wilkinson, New American Library; New York; 1987.

Sports Illustrated Football: Winning Defense; by Bud Wilkinson; New American Library; New York; 1987.

The Super Book of Football; by J. David Miller; *Sports Illustrated For Kids* Books; 1990.

GOLF

Golf is wonderfully suited to a lifetime of fulfilling play. A young golfer can look forward to decades of healthy participation. The threat of injury for kids who play golf is virtually nonexistent, although it's always a good idea to watch out for errant balls and speeding golf carts.

Equipment: A starter set of golf clubs — usually including a Number 3 and Number 5 woods; 3, 5, 7 and 9 irons and a putter, can cost from $75 to $150. Golf shoes with metal spikes on the soles are considered a luxury for young players.

Season: For some people, it's golf season as long as there's no snow on the ground, although most courses in four-season climates do have a prescribed spring-through-fall season.

Fees: Golf is not cheap. "Greens fees" vary and can be substantial, though some public courses offer discounts for players 16 and under, 13 and under, etc. Lessons from a qualified pro can be costly, but golf camps and workshops run privately or by golfing organizations are usually more reasonable. If a junior golfer wants competition, tournament fees ($65-$85 for those run by the American Junior Golf Association) must be paid.

For more information:

Golf; edited by Joseph C. Dey; Boy Scouts of America; North Brunswick, N.J.; 1977.

Golf Basics; by Roger Schiffman; Prentice-Hall; Englewood Cliffs, N.J.; 1986.

Golf is for Me; by Mark Lerner; Lerner Publications; Minneapolis; 1982.

Sports Illustrated Golf: Play Like a Pro; by Mark Mulvoy; New American Library; New York; 1988.

GYMNASTICS

Gymnastics involves a lot of hyperflexion, hyperextension and weight bearing and loading, which result in an inordinate number of overuse injuries, including growth disturbances and lower back problems. Spondylolysis, a relatively common stress fracture in the lower part of the spine, is frequently found in young female gymnasts. Adolescent swayback, a curve in the lower back marked by a protuberant rear end, can result from participation in gymnastics; this causes a marked increase in stress over this area of the spine. Since serious competition starts at an early age, some kids can become too competitive, leaving them prone to psychological and physical burnout. Look at available programs carefully to see if you're comfortable with their level of competition and training techniques.

Equipment: Girls typically wear a leotard and a soft gym shoe or sneaker; boys wear a T-shirt or leotard top and shorts or "whites" — form-fitting pants that cover the feet as well. These must be provided by the parents or kids. Gloves or hand-grips are optional.

Season: Varies depending on locale. Generally, for competitive junior gymnasts, the season runs from Christmas through March or April. For beginning gymnasts the season runs from September through December.

Meets: Depends on the level of competition and number of participants.

Practice: Depends on the level of competition and, more important, the goals of the individual. For instance young gymnasts in a beginners' program might practice twice a week for 2 1/2 hours each time, while more advanced competitors might train five days a week for four hours each session.

Fees: Depends on the level of competition. Memberships in local YMCAs or health clubs may grant automatic use of gymnastics equipment. Some local recreation clubs may require a nominal weekly charge. Private instruction is available but is very expensive.

For more information:

Better Gymnastics for Girls; by George Sullivan; Dodd, Mead; New York; 1977.

The Complete Beginner's Guide to Gymnastics; by Edward F. Dolan; Doubleday; Garden City, N.Y.; 1980.

Gymnastics; by Brian Hayhurst; Rand McNally; Chicago; 1980.

Gymnastics; by Jim and Pauline Prestidge; Rourke; Vero Beach, Fla.; 1984.

Gymnastics and You: The Whole Story of the Sport; by Michael D. Resnick; Rand McNally; Chicago; 1977.

Gymnastics Basics; by John and Mary Jean Traetta; Prentice-Hall; Englewood Cliffs, N.J.; 1979.

Illustrated Gymnastics Dictionary for Young People; by Ila Guraedy; Harvey House; New York; 1980.

Some Basics About Women's Gymnastics; by Ed and Ruth Radlauer; Childrens Press; Chicago; 1980.

ICE HOCKEY

There is a high injury rate among kids who play hockey, particularly in the leagues that allow checking. Since the foot is protected by the skate (which reaches above the ankle), there aren't many ankle injuries.

In contact leagues, however, there are plenty of knee problems (mostly contusions and fractures), as well as head, neck and shoulder injuries (including lots of separated shoulders). Most of these are "checking injuries," which are the result of getting pushed into the boards or onto the ice. There are also strained and torn ligaments and some contusions from flailing sticks (though rarely any eyes poked out). Proper helmets and padding are a must, and the use of eye goggles or shields is also recommended.

Equipment: Skates, a stick, a helmet, face mask (for all players, not just goalies), mouthpiece and pads are required; the cost can run to $100-$150. Because of the expense, used equipment is a popular alternative, provided the skates are not too worn.

Season: Generally from late Fall through February.

Games: Depends on the level of play. Very young players may not play formal games at all, but will scrimmage.

Practice: Depends on the level of play.

Fees: League membership fees are typically $10 per player; the cost of rink time varies by locale.

For more information:

Basic Hockey Strategy; by Richard B. Lyttle; Doubleday; Garden City, N.Y.; 1976.

Checking and Defensive Play; by John Gilbert; Creative Education; Mankato, Minn.; 1976.

The Easy Hockey Book; by Jonah Kalb; Houghton Mifflin; Boston; 1977.

Hockey Basics; by Norman MacLean; Prentice-Hall; Englewood Cliffs, N.J.; 1983.

Hockey for Beginners; by Kevin Walsh; Four Winds Press; New York; 1976.

Hockey is for Me; by Lowell A. Dickmeyer; Lerner Publications; Minneapolis; 1978.

Illustrated Hockey Dictionary for Young People; by Henry Walker; Harvey House; New York; 1976.

Sports Illustrated Hockey: Learn to Play the Modern Way; by Jack Falla; New American Library; New York; 1987.

MARTIAL ARTS

The most common injuries among kids who participate in martial arts are fractures, which are usually the result of kids taking a fall incorrectly, and twisted elbows, wrists or even ankles. The injury rate is often directly proportional to the preparation and competence of the coach (called a *sensei*).

Judo and karate are the two most popular martial arts taught to children in the United States. Judo, an adaptation of ju-jitsu, has been around for about 3,000 years and is best known for its ranking system of belts — from the novice's white to the expert's black, which has additional categories of excellence. Karate techniques began under the influence of Chinese martial arts around A.D. 1500. In the 20th Century they were refined in Japan and spread throughout the world. In competition, basic rules are set by the World Union of Karatedo Organization in Japan governing the use of punching, striking and kicking various parts of the body. As in judo, a rating system of belts is used.

Equipment: For judo, a white robe known as a *judogi* is the only necessity; it costs from $20-$50 (although sometimes they are provided by the judo club). For karate, no robe is required for beginners (white belts), but arm guards, shin guards and athletic supporters (for boys) are needed when you get more advanced.

Season: Judo and karate competitions generally take place during the summer, but both can be practiced recreationally year-round.

Practice: Depends on individual desires and goals. Some beginners practice once a week for an hour or two; other enthusiasts practice three or four days per week, one or two hours per session.

Fees: Depends on the locale. Some YMCAs include lessons with the basic membership cost; others charge a small fee. Most private clubs and camps charge membership fees.

For more information:

Lessons from the Samurai: Ancient Self-Defense Strategies and Techniques; by Fred Neff; Lerner Publications; Minneapolis; 1987.

The Martial Arts; by Norman Barrett; Franklin Watts; London; 1988.

Martial Arts for Young Athletes; by Michael DePasquale; Wanderer Books; New York; 1984.

The Complete Beginner's Guide to Judo; by Stuart James; Doubleday; Garden City, N.Y.; 1978.

Judo is for Me; by John Ralph Holm; Lerner Publications; Minneapolis; 1986.

Karate; by Larry Dane Brimner; Franklin Watts; New York; 1988.

Karate Basics; by Thomas J. Nardi; Prentice-Hall; Englewood Cliffs, N.J.; 1984.

Karate for Young People; by Russell Kozuki; Sterling Publishing; New York; 1974.

Karate Handbook; by J. Allen Queen; Sterling Publishing Co.; New York; 1986.

SKIING

There are two major types of skiing: downhill and cross-country. Downhill is just as it sounds — skiing down slopes of varying degrees of difficulty. Cross-country skiing involves traversing terrain (usually flat) on skis that are narrower than downhill skis. It's done with long, striding motion. The learning process is usually simpler and easier than that for downhill and there are not as many dangers or variables. Still, cross-country skiing is quite rigorous.

There is a high injury rate among downhill skiers, usually from a collision with either an immoveable object or another skier. Twisted knees and fractures are common, although because of the excellent support provided by ski boots (which can virtually hold you up when you stand), skiing injuries almost never include sprained or fractured ankles. Warm, flexible clothing that breathes is a big help. Be sure to get assistance in the proper fit and adjustment of skis and poles.

Equipment: For downhill skiing, a pair of skis, bindings, boots, and poles can cost from $350 to $500. Equipment can also be rented at most ski resorts. If you want to buy equipment, consider buying during the off-season or used equipment. If you plan to participate infrequently, look for discount rentals from sporting-goods stores.

Season: Whenever and wherever there's snow.

Fees: Downhill skiing is an expensive sport; in addition to the cost of buying equipment you must pay for lift tickets, which can run from $30 to $35. Cross-country is less expensive but not cheap.

For more information:

Beginning Cross-Country Skiing; by Margaret Church; Children's Press; Chicago; 1979.

The Complete Beginner's Guide to Skiing; by Richard B. Lyttle; Doubleday; Garden City, N.Y.; 1978.

Cross-Country Skiing is for Me; by Rosemary G. Washington; Lerner Publications; Minneapolis; 1982.

Illustrated Skiing Dictionary for Young People; by Claire Walter; Harvey House; New York; 1980.

Skiing Basics; by Alfred Marozzi; Prentice-Hall; Englewood Cliffs, N.J.; 1980.

Sports Illustrated Cross-Country Skiing: A Complete Guide; by Casey Sheahan; New American Library; New York; 1988.

SOCCER

Soccer is a contact sport in which contusions, sprains and strains are common among players. Fractures are not unheard of. At some levels, leg tackles have been outlawed to prevent injuries. There tend to be more injuries in girls' soccer than in boys' soccer; this is an indication of the level of contact. The use of shin guards can help prevent injuries from kicking.

Equipment: In most youth leagues balls are provided. Uniforms may be bought from the league, usually for a nominal charge of around $15. Parents also pay for soccer shoes (around $40) as well as shin guards, which are often required.

Season: Some communities have two full soccer seasons — fall and spring, while others play in the fall only.

Games: Usually around 10 per season.

Practice: Anywhere from 1-6 hours per week, depending on the kids' ages, availability and the coaches' temperament (and availability).

Fees: Usually around $30-40, depending on the type of league and/or region of the country. A significant part of this fee (about one-third) often includes insurance costs.

For more information:

Be a Winner in Soccer; by Charles Ira Coombs; Pocket Books; New York; 1980.

Better Soccer for Boys and Girls; by George Sullivan; Dodd, Mead; New York; 1978.

Controlling the Ball; by James Rothaus; Children's Book; Mankato, Minn.; 1980.

Goal!: A Soccer Handbook for Young Players; by Paul E. Harris; Soccer for Americans; Manhattan Beach, Calif.; 1977.

How to Play Better Soccer; by C. Paul Jackson; Crowell; New York; 1978.

I Want to Be a Soccer Player; by Eugene H. Baker; Children's Press; Chicago; 1976.

Illustrated Soccer Dictionary for Young People; by James Boyd Gardner; Harvey House; New York; 1976.

Make the Team: Soccer; by Richard J. Brenner; *Sports Illustrated For Kids* Books; 1990.

Soccer; by Edward Radlauer; Children's Press; Chicago; 1978.

Soccer; by Clive Toye; Franklin Watts; New York; 1979.

Soccer Basics; by Alex Yannis; Prentice-Hall; Englewood Cliffs, N.J.; 1982.

Soccer for Young Champions; by Robert J. Antonacci and Anthony J. Puglisi; McGraw-Hill; New York; 1978.

Sports Illustrated Soccer: The Complete Player; by Dan Herbst; New American Library; New York; 1988.

Starting Soccer: A Handbook for Boys and Girls; by Edward F. Dolan, Jr.; Harper & Row; New York; 1976.

Soccer Tips; by David Clements; J. Messner; New York; 1978.

SWIMMING

Swimming is a great sport for overall cardiovascular health. There are very few swimming injuries; most are overuse syndromes, usually affecting the shoulders (particularly as a result of doing the butterfly and freestyle strokes). Breast strokers can develop knee problems from doing the whip kick.

Equipment: A bathing suit, cap and goggles (optional) are all that parents and kids must provide. Kickboards, fins and the like are usually provided by clubs or other swimming organizations.

Season: Swimming — competitive or recreational — takes place year-round, with the April-to-August period a little more active.

Meets: Depends on the level of competition. Some swimmers have meets every three weeks, others less frequently.

Practice: Depends on the level of competition. A routine is considered beneficial, whether one is competing or simply swimming for fitness and fun.

Fees: Depends on the locale. Some clubs charge a monthly fee, others include pool privileges as part of the membership.

For more information:

Better Swimming for Boys and Girls; by George Sullivan; Dodd, Mead; New York; 1982.

The Complete Beginner's Guide to Swimming; by Shaney Frey; Doubleday; Garden City, N.Y.; 1975.

Freestyle Swimming; by Frank Ryan; Viking Press; New York; 1972.

Sports Illustrated Competitive Swimming: Techniques For Champions; by Mark Schubert; New American Library; New York; 1989.

Swimming and Diving; by C.G. Wilson; Silver Burdett; Morristown, N.J.; 1988.

Swimming Basics; by Charles Rob Orr and Jane B. Tyler; Prentice-Hall; Englewood Cliffs, N.J.; 1980.

TENNIS

Tennis is a physically demanding sport, and you should make sure that your child does not play beyond his physiological capabilities. Injuries associated with tennis are Little League Elbow and Tennis Elbow, a strain on the outside of the elbow that usually arises because of an improper backhand swing. For kids to develop these problems, however, they have got to hit a lot of balls and — in most cases — use an improper stroke. Rarely do kids in the 8 to 13 age group sustain these injuries. Foot injuries are relatively uncommon, although there are a few sprained ankles.

Twenty-five years ago, interscholastic tennis teams were usually found only in affluent areas and were offered predominantly on the high school level. Now the sport is available to kids from different economic backgrounds and competition starts in middle school and even earlier.

Equipment: A good racket (from $20 to $40), a can of balls and maybe a decent pair of tennis sneakers are all that's needed — other than a court — to play tennis; two pairs of socks are also recommended. Clothing is a matter of preference. Most clubs no longer require whites (all-white tennis shirt and shorts); some ask for shirts with collars and some have no dress code at all.

Season: Tennis can be played year-round, though access to indoor courts is limited and can be quite expensive.

Practice: Depends on the individual player's goals.

Fees: With the rise in real estate and the shakeout after the tennis boom of the 1970s, the cost of court time has risen. So has the price of quality teaching. Instructional clinics — a group of kids running through drills with one or more qualified pros — is an excellent way to begin learning the game. From there, some kids may want to take it to the next level — either with intensive individual instruction or at a tennis school or camp.

For more information:

Competitive Tennis: A Guide for Parents and Young Players; by David A. Benjamin; Lippincott; New York; 1979.

Net Results: Training the Tennis Parent for Competition; by James E. Loehr; S. Greene Press; Lexington, Mass.; 1987.

Sports Illustrated Tennis: Strokes for Success; by Doug MacCurdy and Shawn Tully; New American Library; New York; 1988.

Teaching Children Tennis the Vic Braden Way; by Vic Braden and Bill Bruns; Little, Brown; Boston; 1980.

Teaching Your Children Tennis; by Bob Huang and Arthur Shay; Contemporary Books; Chicago; 1979.

Tennis and Kids: The Family Connection; by Jim Fannin, with John Mullin; Doubleday; Garden City, N.Y.; 1979.

Tennis Love: A Parents' Guide to the Sport; by Billie Jean King and Greg Hoffman; Macmillan; New York; 1978.

You Can Teach Your Child Tennis; by Carol Kleiman; Popular Library; New York; 1979.

TRACK AND FIELD

Track events include those involved with running (or walking): dashes or sprints (usually beginning at 50 yards) and those over longer distances, up to the marathon. Also included are relays (usually involving four participants handing off a baton over distances usually beginning at 100 yards) and hurdles (jumping over obstacles). The walking races usually cover long distances — up to 50,000 meters.

During a competition, track events usually take place on an oval 440-yard or 400-meter track, while the field events are confined to the area within the oval. Field events include those that involve jumping — as in the high jump, pole vault, long jump and triple jump (hop, skip and jump) — and those that involve throwing — the shotput, discus, hammer and javelin. Kids would normally use lighter-weight objects when competing in these events.

Kids involved in track and field should take care not to overtax their bodies. Marathon running, in particular, is too strenuous for most young athletes. The injuries most commonly associated with track and field are overuse conditions, such as shin splints, jumper's knee, Osgood-Schlatters Disease and Sever's Disease. Occasionally young athletes will sustain acute sprains and strains or fractures.

Equipment: Depends, of course, on the event. In any of the track events, footwear is of primary importance — with different shoes recommended for sprints than for distance races.

Season: Generally spring and summer.

Practice: Depends upon the level of involvement and individual goals.

Fees: Most local track-and-field meets for kids will have a nominal charge (often going to a charity or education fund). Serious competition in this sport doesn't usually begin until high school, though there are major programs in many junior high schools throughout the country.

For more information:

Guide to the Events; by Dan Zadra; Children's Book; Mankato, Minn.; 1981.

Run Faster, Jump Higher, Throw Farther: How to Win at Track and Field; by Louis Sabin; Davis McKay; New York; 1980.

Running Harder; by Donald Honig; Franklin Watts; New York; 1976.

Sports Illustrated Track: Championship Field Events; by Jim Santos and Ken Shannon; New American Library; New York; 1989.

Track and Field Basics; by Fred McMane; Prentice-Hall; Englewood Cliffs, N.J.; 1983.

Track and Field; by Tony Duffy; Silver Burdett; Morristown, N.J.; 1980.

Track is for Me; by Lowell A. Dickmeyer; Lerner Publications; Minneapolis; 1979.

VOLLEYBALL

Volleyball injuries are rare in younger kids, although a few may develop jumper's knee or Osgood-Schlatters Disease. Occasionally there are ankle sprains, usually from landing on a teammate's foot. In addition kids who are on the receiving end of a speedy "spike" can sustain jammed fingers.

Equipment: Traditional gym clothing and sneakers. Nets and balls are provided by the club or gym where the game is played.

Season: Can be played year-round, but most local programs occur during the summer.

Games: Varies by locale and level of play.

Practice: Varies by level of play.

Fees: Some clubs and YMCAs require nominal charges to cover insurance.

For more information:

Basic Volleyball Strategy; by Richard B. Lyttle; Doubleday; Garden City, N.Y.; 1979.

Better Volleyball for Girls; by George Sullivan; Dodd, Mead; New York; 1979.

Volleyball Is for Me; by Art Thomas; Lerner Publications; Minneapolis; 1980.

Part 7
Youth Sports Resources

Here is a grab bag of invaluable resources for the sports-wise parent of athletically active kids.

BASEBALL AND SOFTBALL

Amateur Softball Association
of America
2801 N.E. 50th St.
Oklahoma City, OK 73111
(405) 424-5266

International Softball Federation
2801 N.E. 50th St.
Oklahoma City, OK 73111
(405) 424-6937

Little League Baseball
P.O. Box 3485
Williamsport, PA 17701
(717) 326-1921

Little League Foundation
P.O. Box 3486
Williamsport, PA 17701
(717) 326-1921

National Amateur Baseball Federation
12406 Keynote Ln.
Bowie, MD 20715
(301) 262-0770

Pony Baseball
P.O. Box 225
Washington, PA 15301
(412) 225-1060

COACHING

American Coaching Effectiveness Program
P.O. Box 5076
Champaign, IL 61820
(217) 351-5076

Coaching Association of Canada
333 River Rd.
Ottawa, Ontario
Canada K1L8H9
(613) 748-5624

National Youth Sport Coaches Association
2611 Old Okeechobee Rd.
West Palm Beach, FL 33409
(305) 684-1141

The non-profit NYSCA was formed in 1980 in cooperation with the National Recreation and Park Association. As of 1988 there were 600 chapters of NYSCA nationwide in 43 states; nearly 80,000 coaches have been certified under NYSCA's national certification program.

National Interscholastic Swimming Coaches
  Association of America
c/o Donald R. Allen
Glenbrook South High School
4000 W. Lake Ave.
Glenview, IL 60025
(312) 729-2000

FAMILY SPORTS

American Turners
2503 Preston St.
P.O. Box 17345
Louisville, KY 40217
(502) 636-2395

FIELD HOCKEY

United States Field Hockey Association
1750 E. Boulder St.
Colorado Springs, CO 80909
(719) 578-4567

FITNESS

American Fitness Association
6700 E. Pacific Coast Hwy.
Suite 299
Long Beach, CA 90803
(213) 596-6036

National Association for Sport & Physical Education
1900 Association Drive
Reston, VA 22091
(703) 476-3410

President's Council on Physical Fitness and Sports
450 Fifth St. NW
Suite 7103
Washington, D.C. 20001
(202) 272-3421

PCPFS is the source of many publications and pamphlets, including "The Physically Underdeveloped Child," "Youth Fitness Fact Sheet," "Youth Physical Fitness in 1985," "Two Ways to Join the President's Physical Fitness Team" and "Physical Education: A Performance Checklist."

FOOTBALL

College Football Association
688 Gunpark Dr.
Suite 201
Boulder, CO 80301
(303) 530-5566

Pop Warner Football
1315 Walnut St.
Suite 1632
Philadelphia, PA 19107
(215) 735-1450

GIRLS IN SPORTS

Cinderella Softball Leagues
P.O. Box 1411
Corning, NY 14830
(607) 937-5469

National Association for Girls and Women in Sports
1900 Association Dr.
Reston, VA 22091
(703) 476-3400

Women in Soccer
242 E. 75th St.
New York, NY 10021
(212) 744-1565

Women's Sports Foundation
342 Madison Ave.
Suite 728
New York, NY 10017
(800) 227-3988 (Cannot be used in New York, Alaska and Hawaii)
(212) 972-9170

GOLF

American Junior Golf Association
2415 Steeplechase Ln.
Roswell, GA 30076
(404) 998-4653

Professional Golf Association
112 TPC Blvd.
Ponte Vedra, FL 32082
(904) 285-3700

GYMNASTICS

United States Gymnastics Federation
Pan American Plaza
Suite 300
201 S. Capitol Ave.
Indianapolis, IN 46225
(317) 237-5050

ICE HOCKEY

U.S.A. Hockey
2997 Broadmoor Valley Rd.
Colorado Springs, CO 80906
(719) 576-4990

JUDO

United States Judo Inc.
POB 10013
El Paso, TX 79991
(915) 565-8754

NUTRITION

American Dietetic Association
Sports Nutrition Division
216 W. Jackson
#800
Chicago, IL 60606-6995
(800) 877-1600

International Center for Sports Nutrition
502 S. 44th St.
Suite 3012
Omaha, NB 68105
(402) 559-5505

Source of various pamphlets, including "The Precompetition Meal," "Water, The Most Important Nutrient," "Vitamin and Mineral Supplements," "Carbohydrates" and "Healthy Kids."

PSYCHOLOGY

American Academy of Child and Adolescent Psychiatry
3615 Wisconsin Ave. NW
Washington, DC 20016
(202) 966-7300

Academy of Sports Psychology International
c/o William J. Beausay, Ph.D
6079 Northgate Rd.
Columbus, OH 43229
(614) 846-2275

Institute of Athletic Motivation
One Lagoon Dr.
Suite 141
Redwood, CA 94065
(415) 598-0700

International Society of Sports Psychology
c/o Prof. Glyn C. Roberts
Dept. of Kinesiology
906 S. Goodwin Ave.
University of Illinois at Urbana/Champaign
Urbana, IL 61801
(217) 244-3982

North American Society for the Psychology of Sport and Physical Activity
c/o Mary J. Carlton
Dept. of Kinesiology
906 S. Goodwin Ave.
University of Illinois at Urbana/Champaign
Urbana, IL 61801
(217) 244-3986

SOCCER

National Soccer League
4534 N. Lincoln Ave.
Chicago, IL 60625
(312) 275-2850

Soccer Association for Youth
5945 Ridge Ave.
Cincinnati, OH 45213
(513) 351-7291

United States Youth Soccer Association
1835 Union Ave.
Suite 190
Memphis, TN 38104
(901) 278-7972

SPORTS MEDICINE

American Physical Therapy Association
1111 N. Fairfax St.
Alexandria, VA 22314
(703) 684-2782.

The Physician and Sports Medicine Magazine
4530 W. 77th St.
Minneapolis, MN 55435
(612) 835-3222

Source of a complete list of sports medicine clinics around the country.

U.S. Olympic Committee
Division of Sports Medicine and Science
1750 E. Boulder St.
Colorado Springs, CO 80909

Pamphlets include one on "Sports Nutrition."

SWIMMING

Council for National Cooperation in Aquatics
901 W. New York St.
Indianapolis, IN 46223
(317) 638-4238

United States Swimming, Inc.
1750 E. Boulder St.
Colorado Springs, CO 80909
(719) 578-4578

TENNIS

National Junior Tennis League
USTA Center for Education and Recreational Tennis
729 Alexander Rd.
Princeton, NJ 08540
(609) 452-2580

National Public Parks Tennis Association
3325 Wilshire Blvd.
Suite 604
Los Angeles, CA 90010
(213) 380-7114

National Tennis Foundation and Hall of Fame
100 Park Ave.
2nd Floor
New York, NY 10017
(212) 880-4179

Peter Burwash International Special Tennis Programs
2203 Timberloch Pl.
Suite 126
The Woodlands, TX 77380
(713) 363-4707

VOLLEYBALL

United States Volleyball Association
1750 E. Boulder St.
Colorado Springs, CO 80909
(719) 578-4750

MISCELLANEOUS

Amateur Athletic Union
3400 W. 86th St.
Indianapolis, IN 46268
(317) 872-2900

AAU/Carrier Youth Sports Program
3400 W. 86th St.
P.O. Box 68207
Indianapolis, IN 46268
(317) 872-2900

American Alliance for Health, Physical Education, Recreation and Dance
1900 Association Dr.
Reston, VA 22091
(703) 476-3400

Association of Sports Museums and Halls of Fame
101 W. Sutton Pl.
Wilmington, DE 19810
(302) 475-7068

National Intramural-Recreational Sports Association
Gill Coliseum
Room 221
Oregon State University
Corvallis, OR 97331
(503) 754-2088

National Recreation and Park Association
3101 Park Center Dr.
Alexandria, VA 22302
(703) 820-4940

North American Youth Sport Institute
4985 Oak Garden Dr.
Kernersville, NC 27284
(919) 784-4926

United States Athletes Association
3735 Lakeland Ave. N.
Suite 230
Minneapolis, MN 55422
(612) 522-5844

United States Committee-Sports for Israel
275 S. 19th St.
Suite 1203
Philadelphia, PA 19103
(215) 561-6900

United States Cultural Exchange and Sports Society
P.O. Box 3602
787 N. Woodlawn Dr.
Thousand Oaks, CA 91360
(805) 497-9628

Youth Sport Institute
IM Sports Circle
Michigan State University
E. Lansing, MI 48824
(517) 353-6689

ABOUT THE AUTHOR

Lee R. Schreiber, a New York-based journalist with a diverse portfolio, has worked as an entertainment feature writer and a sports editor at the Associated Press, has written two books on backpacking and was the founding managing editor of *Golf Illustrated*. Recently he has been a contributor to publications such as *The New York Times, Newsweek International, Vis a Vis, Sport, Diversion, New York Newsday, Daily News Sunday Magazine* and *Long Island Monthly*.